VERONA

Palazzo Minischalchi
VERONA.

VERONA

Sheila Hale

Photographs by Mark Smith

Tauris Parke Books, London

The author is particularly grateful to Professor J. R. Hale and Dr Sergio Marinelli for their detailed advice; and to the Banca Popolare di Verona and Museo Castelvecchio, Verona for their generous gifts of books and exhibition catalogues. She would also like to thank Professor Alessandro Bettagno, Dr David Hemsoll and Dr John Law for their help and encouragement.

Published by Tauris Parke Books
110 Gloucester Avenue
London NW1 8JA
In association with KEA Publishing Services Ltd, London

Text © 1991 Sheila Hale
Photographs © 1991 Mark Smith

TRAVEL TO LANDMARKS
Series Editor: Judy Spours
Editorial Assistant: Elizabeth Harcourt
Designers: Holdsworth Associates
Maps by Andras Bereznay
All photographs by Mark Smith except pages 2, 21, 27, 33 *(right)*, 57 *(below)*, 103, 105 *(below)*, 109 *(left)*, 111, 112 *(left)*, 115, 116

British Library Cataloguing in Publication Data
Hale, Sheila
   Verona. – (Travel to landmarks series).
   1. Travel. Italy (Veneto)
   I. Title II. Series
   914.534040929

   ISBN 1-85043 225-2

Photosetting by Litho Link Ltd, Welshpool, Powys, UK
Colour separation by Fabbri, Milan, Italy
Printed by Fabbri, Milan, Italy

Frontispiece Ruskin's watercolour sketch of Palazzo Miniscalchi, probably done in 1845 on the third of his twelve visits to Verona between 1835 and 1888. Photograph: Ruskin Galleries, Bembridge School, Isle of Wight.

Contents

Introduction

Verona, the ancient world-renowned city, situated on both sides of the Adige, has been in all ages the first halting-place for the great German emigrations of tribes which left their cold Northern forests and crossed the Alps, to rejoice in the golden sunshine of pleasant Italy . . . and made themselves at home and comfortable in it, put on their silk dressing gowns and promenaded cheerfully among flowers and cypresses, until newcomers, who still had on their iron garments, arrived from the North and crowded them away – an oft-repeated tale, and one called by historians the emigration of races.

Heine, 1828

The apse and tower of the church of San Fermo Maggiore seen from the Adige. San Fermo was an early Christian martyr who was decapitated on the bank of the river. The Gothic building is superimposed on an earlier church, now below ground level.

The River Adige, running fast out of the Austrian Alps into Italy, flows parallel with the eastern shore of Lake Garda. The Baldo hills above its right bank are carpeted with herbs, wild flowers and lush pastures. The Lessini mountains which rise from the left bank are made of limestones and marbles so various in colour and composition that they have been called the mother of the science of geology; vineyards, orchards and olives flourish in the morainic soil of the valleys. At the village of Pescantina, named for its good fishing, the river sweeps eastwards past the entrance to the Valpolicella and describes a rapid double loop where the Alps, and the most accessible route through them from Germany, meet the broad belt of the fertile Po plains that cross the Italian peninsula from the French border to the Adriatic.

Although the political boundary of modern Italy lies further to the north, most travellers who cross the Brenner Pass and follow the Adige to Verona feel that the real Italy begins here, on the protective curves of the rushing river where the rosy marble city revolves around its vast oval Roman amphitheatre.

Goethe, who crossed the Brenner in 1786 and experienced at Verona his first palpable contact with Italian civilization, was so struck by the seductive rhythm of life in a city 'where everyone enjoys the day but the evening even more' that he drew a diagram to help him adjust to the delectably unfamiliar Italian way of counting and passing the hours:

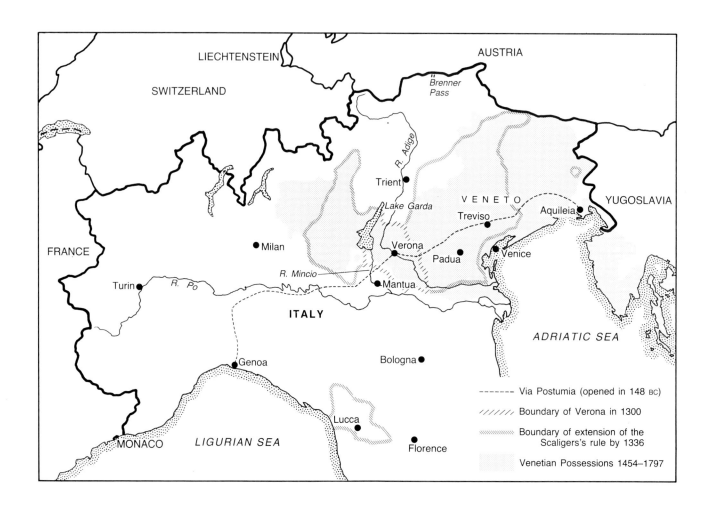

LIECHTENSTEIN

AUSTRIA

SWITZERLAND

"Brenner
Pass"

R. Adige

Trient ●

V E N E T O

YUGOSLAVIA

Lake Garda

Treviso ●

Aquileia ●

FRANCE

● Milan

Verona ●

Padua ●

Venice ●

R. Mincio

Turin ●

R. Po

● Mantua

ITALY

ADRIATIC SEA

● Genoa

Bologna ●

Lucca ●

MONACO ●

LIGURIAN SEA

Florence ●

- - - - - - Via Postumia (opened in 148 BC)

/////// Boundary of Verona in 1300

Boundary of extension of the
Scaligers's rule by 1336

Venetian Possessions 1454–1797

Verona seen from the archaeological museum above the auditorium of the Roman theatre. Writing about the Roman theatre in the sixteenth century the architect Sebastiano Serlio exclaimed: 'It stupifies me even to think of it. And it is understandable that the Romans built like this in Verona: because it has in my view the most beautiful situation in Italy.' The theatre was originally approached from across the Adige by a pair of bridges, of which only the Ponte di Pietra survives. Beyond the Ponte de Pietra is the bell tower of the cathedral. The towers in the distance on the left are those of the church of San Zeno. On the right is the dome of the church of San Giorgio in Braida.

'We Cimmerians hardly know the real meaning of day. With our perpetual fogs and cloudy skies we do not care if it is day or night . . . If one were to force a German clock hand on them, they would be at a loss, for their own method of time measurement is closely bound up with their nature.' Of the amphitheatre, 'the first great monument of the ancient world I have seen,' he exclaimed: 'and how well preserved it is!'

Verona was founded by the Romans a little over two thousand years ago. It was one of the most beautiful of all ancient cities, and when the Roman Empire collapsed successive waves of invaders from the north were impressed, charmed and tamed by the magnificence of its classical buildings, its strategic location, and the superabundant fertility of the surrounding countryside. Far from razing and pillaging, as they went on to do in other Roman cities, they acted as Verona's caretakers, setting a preservationist tradition which has persisted ever since. Aspects of northern Europe material culture were gradually grafted on to the antique roots, resulting in a balanced and mutually enriching fusion of Roman and Teutonic.

Many of Verona's landmarks are exceptional. The Arena is the third largest and most architecturally unusual of surviving Roman amphitheatres, and the only one apart from the Colosseum to stand at the hub of a modern city; the church of San Zeno is among the most moving of Romanesque religious buildings; the elaborate splendour of the Scaliger lords' gothic tombs and the muscular magnificence of the Renaissance city gates are unrivalled in Italy; the eighteenth-century customs house has no parallel in the Veneto. And yet, although the buildings span two millennia and a variety of styles and influences from both sides of the Alps, they are as remarkable for their common characteristics as for their individual importance.

Verona is chiefly built of marbles quarried from its mountainous backdrop. All of Verona's builders, from the humblest anonymous stonemasons to the greatest named architects, have shared a sensuous, almost painterly, appreciation of the colour and texture of the local materials, of the way they interact and respond to skilled carving. The eye is constantly distracted in Verona by decorative detail – the quality and rich elaboration of the carving surrounding a doorway, the curve or spring of a gothic or Roman arch.

The streets are paved with pink and ivory marble slabs; the buildings are made of finely laid rose bricks, soft limestones and marbles that

The top section of the Torre dei Lamberti, raised from its Romanesque base in the 1460s. It is the oldest and tallest tower in Verona (see page 45).

range in colour from crisp white to peaches and cream, warm reds and vivid lavenders shot with bronze. The variegated marbles from the higher reaches of the Lessini are 'so rich and grotesque in their veinings, and so fancifully lending themselves to decoration' that John Ruskin, who wrote some of his most ecstatic prose about Verona and its quarries, found himself wondering after all whether the buildings were real buildings 'or only museums of practical geology'.

But for all its rich surface decoration, Verona's most characteristic architecture has a robust masculinity that reflects the role as garrison city in which geography and history cast it from the days of the Roman Empire to the Austrian occupation in the first half of the nineteenth century. It has always been a conservative city, more concerned with civic self-definition than with innovation, where successive generations of builders have looked over their shoulders with admiring respect completing, re-interpreting or quoting verbatim the work of their predecessors.

The amphitheatre is not only the city's centrepiece. It is the emblem of the most intact Roman city outside Rome itself, the keynote of that city's neo-Roman architecture, and a manifesto of the civic values that continue even today to breathe life into the old classical bones of one of the loveliest cities in Europe.

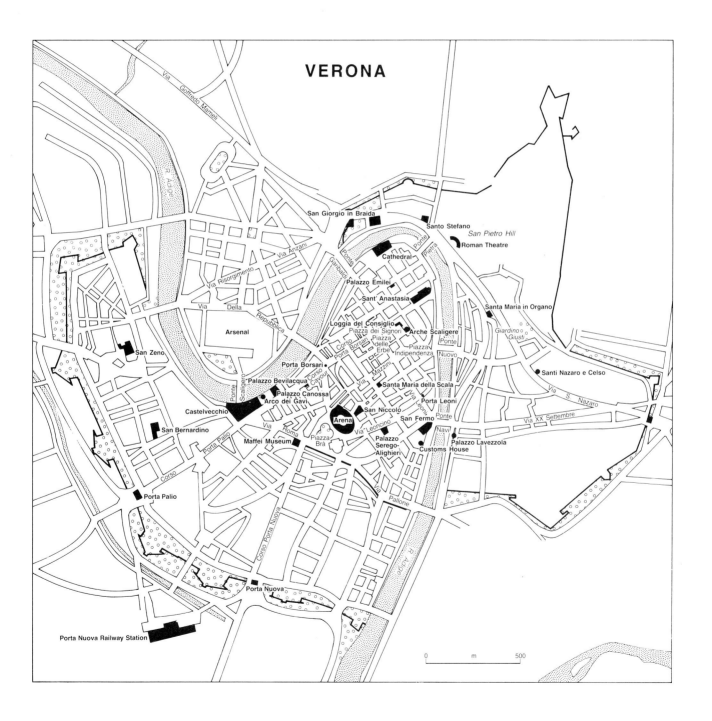

VERONA

San Giorgio in Braida

Santo Stefano

San Pietro Hill

Roman Theatre

Cathedral

Palazzo Emilei

Sant' Anastasia

Santa Maria in Organo

Via Anzani

Via Risorgimento

Via Della

Repubblica

Arsenal

Loggia del Consiglio

Piazza dei Signori

Piazza delle Erbe

Arche Scaligere

Giardino Giusti

Corso Borsari

Piazza Indipendenza

Ponte Nuovo

San Zeno

Porta Borsari

Santi Nazaro e Celso

Via S. Nazaro

Palazzo Bevilacqua

Corso Cavour

Santa Maria della Scala

Palazzo Canossa

Arco dei Gavi

Via Leoni

Porta Leoni

Castelvecchio

Via Mazzini

San Niccolo

San Fermo

Via XX Settembre

Via Roma

Arena

San Bernardino

Via Leoncino

Navi

Palazzo Lavezzola

Maffei Museum

Piazza Brà

Palazzo Serego-Alighieri

Customs House

Porta Palio

Corso

Corso Porta Nuova

Via Pallone

R. Adige

Porta Palio

Porta Nuova

Porta Nuova Railway Station

0   m   500

R. Adige

Via Golfredo Mameli

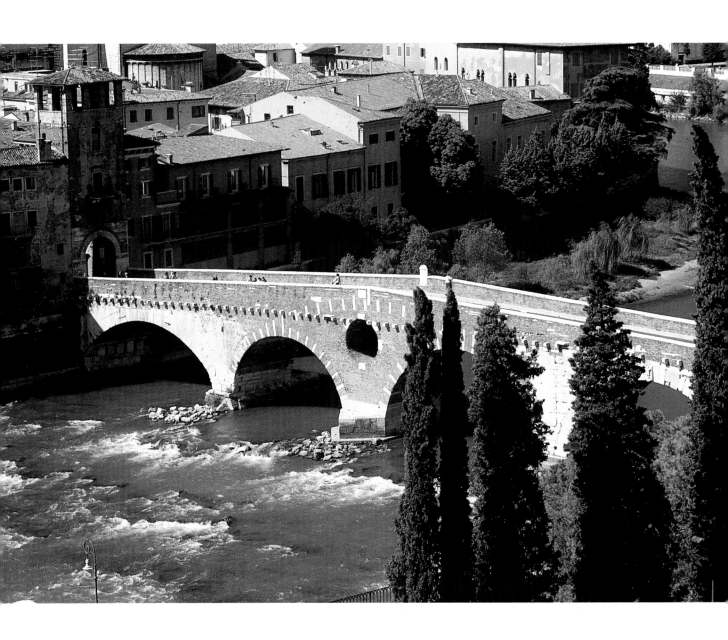

1 Roman and Early Medieval Verona

The inhabitants of Verona have always distinguished themselves by an unusual attachment to their ancient monuments . . . Such zeal and attention . . . afford an honourable proof that they not only boast of Roman extraction, but retain some features of the Roman character.

The Reverend John Chetwode Eustace, *Classical Italy*, 1812

Left Ponte di Pietra, the 'stone bridge', spans the Adige at its narrowest point. This bridge, which antedates the Roman city, is the oldest standing monument in Verona.

Overleaf The centrepiece of Verona is the Roman amphitheatre known as the Arena. It was built around 30 AD and is today the third largest surviving Roman amphitheatre and the only one, apart from the Colosseum in Rome, to stand at the centre of a modern city.

Verona and its territory were inhabited at least from the fifth century BC by an increasingly rich mixture of peoples: Rhaetians from the Tyrolean Alps, Gauls, Veneti, Euganeans and finally Cimbri, the first of the Teutonic tribes to migrate from north Germany to Italy. The nucleus of these early settlements may have been on the hill of San Pietro, which rises steeply from the north bank of the Adige and is now capped by a massive nineteenth-century Austrian barrack. But when the Romans came to build the city, they laid it out with such ruthless efficiency that all but a few fragmentary traces of previous civilizations were destroyed.

The Roman presence in Verona begins in 148 BC with the opening of the Via Postumia, the Roman road that crossed the Italian peninsula from Genoa to the north coast of the Adriatic. At Verona the Via Postumia crossed the Adige by way of a wooden bridge and followed the course of an earlier road of which traces have been discovered under the modern Via Cavour. Wealthy and cultivated Roman families built villas along its fringes, enjoyed the beauty of the situation and grew even wealthier from the agriculture and commerce of the region. Indeed, these have been the mainstays of the economy ever since. Virgil praised the Rhaetic wines grown on the hills to the north. The Roman lyric poet, Catullus, was born near Verona shortly after 80 BC.

Verona, however, was a market town but not yet a city when Catullus died in 54 BC. The only surviving monument that he would have known is the Ponte Pietra, which crosses the Adige at its narrowest point and where the embankments are strongest. The appearance of this bridge, which antedates the Roman colony and is not aligned to its rigorously logical street plan, is the result of frequent restorations undertaken from the second century AD, and possibly earlier.

The foundation of the Roman city is announced by an inscription (rediscovered in 1959) on a pier of the Porta Leoni, the brick gate near the eastern leg of the Adige. The inscription, which instructs the magistrates of the municipality to build walls, gates and drains, can be dated between 49 and 42 BC, that is in the late Republican period at the time when Roman citizenship was extended beyond the Po as far as the foothills of the Alps and *Venetia et Histria* became one of the ten regions of Roman Italy. Although there is no certain evidence that the city was founded before the death of Julius Caesar in 44 BC, Verona has always thought of itself as 'Caesar's city'.

Verona knew its first golden age after 16 BC when a successful war waged by the Emperor Augustus against the Alpine populations secured the northern boundaries of Roman Italy. Towards the end of the first century AD Imperial Verona was described by the Latin epigrammatist Martial as an unusually large city and by the historian Tacitus as populous and important. North Italy was at the head of a rapidly expanding empire and Verona was located at the intersection of its most frequented trading routes. Labour was cheap. There was a lot of new money around; and money could buy social rank and satisfy the gargantuan Roman appetite for public entertainment. The city soon sprawled beyond its walls, and the luxuriousness of villas which have been excavated in the suburbs and surrounding countryside indicate a thriving market economy. The happiest years were during the reigns of the Emperors Claudius (AD 41–54) and Nero (AD 54–68). After a century of peace and with no imminent fear of enemy invasion, the walls ceased to serve a practical defensive purpose; the façades of the city gates were elegantly renewed, and the Via Postumia, outside the western walls, was lined with temples and triumphal arches.

After a mild recession early in the second century, the economy – judging by the quality and extent of domestic building and restoration – seems to have picked up and remained steady: until the following century when the Empire began to crack apart under the strain of political and military instability, rampant inflation and chaotic reaction to the threat of invasion by Teutonic tribes from north of the Alps.

Verona's strategic location at the throat of one of the most accessible routes into Italy from Germany made it a key in the defence line that was thrown across northern Italy by the Emperor Gallienus. The city's honorary title, Colonia Augusta, was hastily renewed by central

government in Rome – the first but not the last time in its long history that Verona would be flattered into complying with the military policy of a foreign master. In 265, by order of Gallienus, the old brick Republican walls, which had fallen into disrepair after three centuries of uninterrupted peace, were rebuilt in the short space of nine months, between April and December. They were extended, by only ten metres, to embrace the amphitheatre, which could have served invaders as a fortress. The densely populated suburbs were ruthlessly excluded.

A section of these walls, with the 'Gallienus' bar tucked conveniently into it, stands behind the amphitheatre. They were 14 metres high, and the first 7 metres were constructed with whatever stone came to hand: slabs of marble street paving, blocks taken from the necropoli and public buildings including the theatre and amphitheatre. This was the last great public building project of Imperial Verona, and it wreaked more destruction in nine months than the barbarians who, as we shall see, turned out to be unexpectedly civilized when they finally arrived. Indeed, the cult of antiquity in Verona, and the extraordinary story of the preservation of the city's Roman heritage, began as the power and influence of Rome declined.

Thanks partly to those barbarians, Verona is today the most intact Roman city outside Rome itself. And its state of preservation is all the more remarkable when one compares it to other Italian towns and cities, some three-quarters of which have Roman foundations which scarcely reveal themselves above ground. In the Renaissance, the quantity, the exceptional quality and the idiosyncracy of its antique monuments, some of which are stylistically unique, served Italian architects as a repository of classical motifs which they borrowed and applied to their own cities. The buildings of Alberti, Peruzzi, the Sangallos, Sebastiano Serlio and Palladio are all informed, to a greater or lesser degree, by Roman Verona. The great native Renaissance architects, Fra Giocondo, Falconetto and Michele Sanmicheli, who cut their teeth on Verona's Roman monuments, were the pioneers of Classical architecture in the Veneto.

The first analytical study of Roman Verona, entitled *De amplitudine et antiquitae civitatis Veronae*, published in 1540, is written in the form of a dialogue and is extensively illustrated by Giovanni Caroto. Further investigations were conducted in the eighteenth century, notably by the Enlightenment scholar and antiquarian Scipione Maffei, and at

The Arena originally consisted of four concentric oval rings. The outer ring was entirely constructed of blocks of red limestone from the Valpolicella. The four surviving bays of this outer ring are known as the 'ala', or wing.

Tav. X.

Above A sixteenth-century reconstruction on paper of the Porta Leoni drawn by Giovanni Caroto. Photograph: The British Architectural Library, RIBA, London.

Left The remains of the Roman Porta Leoni, the 'Lion Gate' as it was later called, near the eastern leg of the Adige. The brick gate was built shortly after 50 BC. An inscription recording the foundation of the Roman city was found on it in 1959. The more elaborate stone façade was superimposed on the original brick gate in about 40 AD.

intervals throughout the nineteenth and early twentieth centuries. But it is only recently that the results of the first fully scientific, modern programme of excavations carried out in the 1980s have made it possible to reconstruct with some certainty the original appearance of the standing antique fragments and to locate others buried below the modern city.

The centrepiece of modern Verona is, of course, the Arena, the third largest Roman amphitheatre in Italy after those at Rome and Capua; and the only one, apart from the Colosseum, to stand at the hub of a modern Italian city. The Arena is to Verona what Brunelleschi's cranium-shaped cathedral dome is to Florence: almost alarmingly out of scale with its surroundings, a Brobdingnagian manifesto of civic values. Brunelleschi worked out how to rival Roman technology. But Verona, unlike Florence, preserved its original Roman buildings.

The original audience capacity of the amphitheatre, which was built to seat some 28–30 000 people (that is 5000 more than today), gives some idea of the population of Verona and its suburbs when it was completed around 30 AD. It stood outside the Republican city walls, with its principal ceremonial entrance on the north-west facing the city. The dead and wounded victims of gladiator fights, wild-animal hunts and boxing matches were carried out through the gate facing the country on the south-east. The building consisted of four oval rings, the outermost axis measuring 152 × 123 metres. The exterior ring, of which only the four bays known as the 'ala', or wing, survive, was entirely constructed of great rusticated blocks of red limestone from the Valpolicella which were cut approximately to size in the quarries and transported to the site by oxcart. At ground level there were 72 barrel vaults framed by pilasters with the same number of arches on each of the next two stories. All three stories were composed in the Tuscan order, which was rarely used on Roman buildings except in Verona.

The Arena was partly spoiled to provide building materials for Gallienus' walls. Two earthquakes in the twelfth century caused further structural damage. But from the thirteenth century onwards preservation orders were zealously enforced. The present interior arrangement is the result of a carefully considered restoration carried out in the sixteenth century, a time when the robust magnificence of its rustication and tough, military spring of its arches also exerted a major influence on the architecture of the city as it was then being rebuilt.

Some scholars believe that Dante, who knew Verona very well in the fourteenth century – when the Arena was used for public executions – may have modelled the topography of his Inferno, which consists of similar tiers of descending concentric circles, on this amphitheatre. It has been a compulsory landmark for foreign tourists at least since the seventeenth century when Italy became the highpoint for classically educated British visitors on the Grand Tour, although not all have made such exalted literary use of it as Dante. Here, for instance, is Thomas Coryatt's bathetically calculating reaction in 1608: 'Were such a building to be made in England, I thinke it would cost at the least two millions of our pounds, that is, twenty hundred thousand pound, even as much as tenne of our fayrest Cathedrall Churches.' John Evelyn, writing in 1646, esteemed it 'one of the noblest Antiquities in Europ, worth the seeing . . . having escaped the ruines of other publique buildings for above 1400 Yeares'. Byron in an irritable letter of 1816 which was mainly devoted to debunking the spurious trappings of the Romeo and Juliet legend, could not resist adding: 'The amphitheatre is wonderful – beats even Greece.' Henry James, after an afternoon spent 'beneath the kindly sky and upon the sun-warmed stones' of the Arena, wrote that he had never before 'felt so keenly the difference between the background to life in very old and very new civilizations'.

To the north of the Arena the city was contained within the peninsula formed by the broad, protective curve of the Adige. The brick Republican walls ran along the inner sides of the present Via Leoncino and Via Cantore. The ancient gridded street plan is still clearly visible from the air, and still partly determines that of the modern centre, where some blocks are identical in size to the Roman *insulae*. The axes of the two main streets, the decumano maximus and cardo maximus, are traced respectively by the Corso Porta Borsari – Corso Sant'Anastasia and the Via Leoni – Via Cappello.

The Via Postumia intersected with the Via Gallica to the south-west of the centre, where the Castelvecchio now stands, and entered the city through the Porta Borsari (so called since the Middle Ages when it was used as a toll and customs gate). Only the outward-facing façade remains of what was originally a large building, 13 metres high and 17.8 metres deep, which served the Romans as barrack outstation and customs post. The original Republican gate, if there was one, has been

Via Cappello follows the course of the Roman cardo maximus which ran straight across the city from the Porta Leoni to the Forum. The street is seen here from the excavated base of one of the polygonal defence towers of the Porta Leoni. The Torre dei Lamberti is in the background.

lost. The existing façade, built of white marble some time in the AD 40s, consists of three superimposed orders, the ground level composed of a twin pair of barrel vaults framed by fluted Corinthian half-columns supporting the entablature and dentillated pediments. These features are reassembled nearby on the façade of the sixteenth-century Palazzo Bevilacqua and elsewhere in Verona.

The cardo maximus started from the opposite edge of the city at the Porta Leoni. The first, late-Republican gate measured 16.7 square metres and enclosed a rectangular central courtyard flanked by two galleries. Two large polygonal defence towers rose from the corners of the southern façade facing the Adige. The excavated base of one can be seen in the Corticella Leoni. The northern façade, then facing the city but now incorporated into a later building in the narrow Via Corticella Leoni, was architecturally austere and concluded on its third level with a plain Doric loggia.

About eighty years later – shortly after the completion of the Porta Borsari – a new, richly decorated and architecturally eccentric façade was superimposed on the Republican gate in blocks of white stone from the Lessini Mountains. Only half of this later façade remains. Like the Porta Borsari its vaulted entrances were flanked by fluted Corinthian half-columns. More unusual was the upper loggia with a recessed bay at its centre and supported by four slender columns (only one survives) incised with the twisted fluting that gave energy to the vertical thrust of the architectural ensemble and was later frequently copied in Verona.

The cardo ran from the Porta Leoni to the Forum, now the Piazza delle Erbe. The Forum was a perfect rectangle, larger than the elliptical Piazza. It was paved with large slabs of pink and white marble from the Valpolicella, which are unscarred by chariot wheels indicating that it was probably closed to wheeled traffic, as indeed it is today. Shops on the north-east side preserve, as their basements, their Roman antecedents. The Capitol rose just beyond the junction of the two main thoroughfares at the north-west end of the Forum. The site of the Capitol was rediscovered and extensively excavated in 1983 but has left no traces above ground.

Although the suburb immediately outside the Porta Borsari was scheduled for development early in the first century AD, the only structure in this area to have survived intact is the Arco dei Gavi. This four-sided arch served several purposes: as a subsidiary city gate at a

The fountain in Piazza delle Erbe. 'Madonna Verona', as she is misleadingly called, is in fact a Roman statue which may originally have stood in the Roman baths. She was resurrected in the late fourteenth century by Cansignorio Della Scala who had the fountain built for the use of the merchants. Fresh water was brought to the fountain by lead pipes.

crossroads, as the private mausoleum of the Gavi family and as a triumphal arch celebrating their wealth and prestige. The family was permitted to build it (at their own expense) in return for previous acts of public charity. Some of their names are inscribed below the niches that contained their portrait statues. A short stretch of the original surface of the Via Postumia, heavily scored by chariot wheels, runs beneath the arch.

In the Renaissance the Arco dei Gavi – like the other Roman monuments – was a much consulted source of architectural themes. Many fifteenth-century portals and altarpieces in Verona follow the curve of its archivolts (the door mouldings of two houses, one in Via Sant'Egidio, the other in Via Santa Maria in Chiavica, are exact copies). And in the sixteenth century the local nobility built their altar-tombs in the form of triumphal arches inspired by that of the Gavi.

In the early Renaissance the name of its architect – Vitruvius – conferred an extra, almost mystical, significance on the Arco dei Gavi. In the first century BC Vitruvius Pollio was the author of an architectural treatise which, because it was the only one to survive from antiquity, became the rule-book for Classical Renaissance architects. His name is inscribed twice on the Arco dei Gavi. The inscription high on the left pilaster now facing the Adige, reads: L – VITRVVIUS – LL CERDO – ARCHITECTVS. In the fifteenth century this was taken to mean that the architect L(ucius) Vitruvius Cerdo was a freed slave – LL(ibertus) – of descendants of Vitruvius Pollio, who must therefore have been a citizen of Verona.

The theory, now discredited, had already aroused some scepticism in the High Renaissance. But it captured the imagination of, among others, Andrea Mantegna who copied the inscription in his Eremetani frescoes in Padua. And when the city fathers built their new town hall, the Loggia del Consiglio, at the end of the fifteenth century, a statue of Vitruvius was placed on its roofline with those of other famous Romans – Catullus, Pliny the Younger, Emilius Macrus, Cornelius Nepote (Catullus is the only one now thought to have been a native of Verona). Incidentally, the Arco dei Gavi inscription also set the fashion in Verona and elsewhere in Italy for architects to carve their names on finished works.

The Arco di Giovio Ammone was the other Roman mausoleum/triumphal arch that remained standing outside the Porta Borsari in the

A reconstruction on paper of the Roman theatre drawn by Giovanni Caroto in the sixteenth century shows the two bridges that originally approached the theatre and the temple that crowned the hill above where an Austrian barrack now stands.

sixteenth century and to which Verona's Renaissance architecture also frequently refers. It was dismantled in the seventeenth century to make way for the construction of an inn; and all that remains of it today is the keystone of one arch, sculpted as the effigy of Giovio Ammone, as well as drawings by Caroto, Palladio and the eighteenth-century architect Luigi Trezza.

Through traffic passing under the triumphal arches along the Via Postumia to the theatre entered the city through the Porta Borsari, followed the decumano between the Capitol and Forum and crossed the Adige by way of the Ponte Postumia (now demolished), which ran parallel to the Ponte Pietra. The theatre, approached by its pair of bridges, occupied the whole of the hillside of San Pietro, and was thus the monumental background to the rest of the city. As a scenic ensemble it was unmatched in north Italy, and may have been built by a team of experts from central Italy, where the reticulated brickwork used for some of the walls was also more common than in the north. It was a major engineering feat, even by Roman standards.

The façade, in tufa with architectonic elements picked out in white marble, consisted of three stories, Tuscan at ground level, Ionic above.

The tiered seats of the auditorium were supported by the slope of the hill and by lateral walls vaulted in cement. Above the theatre itself two superimposed galleries were partly cut into the rock (they are now incorporated into the former Convent of San Girolamo); then a system of terraces extended all the way to the top of the hill which was flattened and from which there rose a temple (where the Austrian barrack now stands).

Although probably projected as part of the Republican urban plan, the theatre was not completed until towards the end of the first century AD. After the collapse of the Roman regime it was plundered for stone, shaken by earthquakes and buried under subsequent Christian buildings, fortresses and their debris. Enough was left in the sixteenth century, however, to inspire Andrea Palladio, among others, to make detailed reconstructions on paper. Archaeologists can tell us more about the way the theatre was constructed and the exact measurements of its parts than Palladio and his contemporaries knew. But we see less of the monument that prompted Sebastiano Serlio, in 1540, to exclaim: 'It stupifies me even to think of it. And it is understandable that the Romans built like this in Verona: because it has in my view the most beautiful situation in Italy.'

Early Christian Verona

The Gallienus defence line, which stretched across northern Italy from the Adriatic to Milan, did in fact deflect the barbarians for a time. In 312, however, Constantine the Great unexpectedly crossed the Adige above Verona and all Italy opened to him. The following year his declaration extending toleration to Christians ushered in a new era for Italy.

Verona seems to have taken quickly to the Christian faith. Although the martyrdom of Saints Fermo and Rustico, who were decapitated on the banks of the Adige in 361, indicates that the population was still largely pagan, we know that the city was one of the earliest episcopal seats because San Zeno, who died around 372, was already its eighth Bishop. San Zeno was African and is therefore usually portrayed with a black skin. He was also a keen angler – hence the fish that often dangles from his crozier – as well as a classical scholar, a fine rhetorician and an influential theologian, being the first Latin to insist on the virginity of Mary both before and after the birth of Christ.

Porta Borsari. The exterior façade of the Imperial Roman gate that gave access to the city from the Via Postumia and the west. Like all surviving Roman monuments its architectural components were often quoted by Renaissance architects. The gate takes its name from its use as a toll gate in the Middle Ages. It now marks the entrance to the traffic-free zone of the historic centre.

His ninety-three sermons give a vivid picture of the ecclesiastical practice and daily life of his day; and his own life-story is the subject of a rustic, popular verse-narrative written in the eighth century to be sung. Some of the miracles he performed are depicted on the doors of the beautiful Romanesque church that was built and dedicated to him eight centuries after his death. They include the exorcising of the daughter of Gallienus, from whose mouth a demon issues.

Such an engaging and civilized man could only have flourished in a relatively orderly society. Verona was spared the full weight of the waves of barbaric devastation that ravaged the splendid Roman cities on the shores of the Adriatic and drove their inhabitants to take refuge

A detail of the Porta Borsari showing the fluted Corinthian columns and twin dentillated pediments of the first of its three stories. These features are re-assembled nearby on the façade of the sixteenth-century Palazzo Bevilacqua and in the Pellegrini Chapel of the church of San Bernardino.

in the Venetian lagoon. The surrounding countryside, however, did suffer from the invasion of the Visigoths at the end of the fourth century. A poem written around the year 400 by the Roman poet Claudian, who followed the defensive campaigns against the Visigoth conqueror Alaric, is set near Verona in what had been an idyllic rustic landscape. It describes the reactions of a simple old smallholder to the destruction of the sources of his livelihood and innocent pleasures by the furious forces unleashed by a war he cannot understand.

In 493, Theoderic the Ostrogoth became King of Italy, which he ruled efficiently until 526, bringing peace, for a time, to the peninsula. Although his official seat was at Ravenna, he was so attached to Verona that he went down in German legend as Theoderic of Verona; and Verona was known in Germany as Theoderic's City (Dietrichs Bern) until the late Middle Ages. He subscribed to the Arian doctrine that Christ was not truly divine, and he went down in local history as a great but evil prince. His story as embroidered over the centuries was doubtless all the more charismatic for its sinister, heretical associations. Legends attached to Theoderic were still in circulation in the fourteenth century. He was credited with having founded and built the entire city, or at least the amphitheatre, which was called the casa di Teoderico. He does seem to have sustained the fabric and traditions of the Roman city, and may have been the first to restore the amphitheatre.

When the Lombards descended into Italy in 568 their King, Alboin, chose Verona as his chief residence. He seems to have been a cruel and intemperate man. According to some chroniclers he was assassinated by his wife whom he had forced to drink from a chalice made from her father's skull. And so began the least civilized period in Verona's history. The Lombards were not distinguished architects and the only significant material testimony of their presence are the two hoards of goldsmiths' work discovered in 1906 and 1964 which are now on display in the Castelvecchio Museum.

Under the Franks, who succeeded the Lombards in 774, Verona enjoyed a political and cultural renaissance. Charlemagne's son, the Frankish king Pépin, made Verona his principal seat. The tradition of classical scholarship, which had never entirely died out in Verona, was exemplified by the archdeacon Pacifico, who died around 846 and whose cultural contributions to the city, including a gift to the cathedral library of 280 manuscripts, are itemized on his epitaph in the cathedral.

'The Italian Epitaphs are often more extravagant than those of other Countries, as the Nation is more given to Compliments and Hyperbole,' sniffed the ever-complacent Addision on seeing this epitaph early in the eighteenth century. Nevertheless, this extraordinary proto-humanist devotion to classical learning was part of the culture that had so painstakingly preserved the antique monuments that the classically educated Addision and his contemporaries came to admire.

In the political and religious turmoil that followed the break-up of Charlemagne's empire in 888 Verona remained loyal to the German Emperors and often held open the door of Italy to German negotiators and armies seeking to regain control over the Italian peninsula. The German connection, which was not finally severed until the sixteenth century, affected the city's art and architecture as well as its political policies throughout the Middle Ages. Verona was the forge of a dual culture, the balanced and mutually enriching mix of Roman and Teutonic that gives the city its particular fairy-tale character and is still reflected by the name of its largest piazza, Piazza Brà. Brà is a shortened from of *braida*, that is *breit*, the German for 'large'.

The Early Medieval Cityscape

The *Iconografia di Raterio*, a bird's-eye view of Verona, drawn by a primitive but punctilious artist towards the close of the millennium, gives a precious impression of the medieval cityscape at that time. The Roman monuments determine and dominate the composition of the drawing. The Arena, with Gallienus' walls still wrapped round it, is in the left-hand corner, balanced on the right by the Porta Leoni flanked by its guard towers; in the centre is the Ponte Pietra, neatly labelled *Pons marmoreus*. The rest of the city is barely recognizable – a jumble of towers, churches, narrow houses and gabled roofs most of which were later demolished by fire, flood, earthquake and war, although the decapitated bosses of some very early medieval towers are squeezed in among the later buildings around the perimeter of Piazza delle Erbe.

It is only recently that archaeologists and urban historians have attempted to piece together a picture of how the structure of the city evolved over the long and eventful post-Roman period. No traces survive of the walls, aqueducts and baths that Theoderic is supposed to have built, or of his palace on the hill of San Pietro. There is, however, plenty of material evidence that the Roman style of domestic houses

Right Arco dei Gavi. The mausoleum of the wealthy Roman Gavi family, constructed in the early first century AD, also served as a triumphal arch at a crossroads outside the western entrance to the city. The name of its architect, Vitruvius, is inscribed on the gate. In the Renaissance this Vitruvius was thought to be a descendant of the influential Roman architectural writer, who was therefore assumed to have been a native of Verona. The gate was demolished by Napoleon and reassembled in 1932 on its present site overlooking the Adige near the Castelvecchio.

Far right A drawing by Palladio of the Arco di Giovio Ammone, another Roman mausoleum/triumphal arch that remained standing outside the Porta Borsari in the sixteenth century and which was closely studied by Renaissance architects. It was demolished in the seventeenth century to make way for an inn. Photograph: The British Architectural Library, RIBA, London.

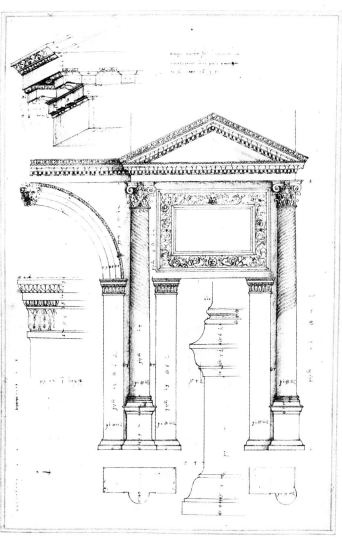

remained fashionable under the Ostrogoths: some fourth-century houses with fine mosaic floors were still inhabited in 600; others were built on the same model in the late fifth century.

Shortly after the arrival of the Lombards the city centre was devastated by fire. In the area in and around the present Tribunal courtyard Roman houses were abandoned and the land continued to be used for agricultural purposes until the eleventh century. Elsewhere, wooden houses were built into the shells of earlier stone structures, and mosaic floors were increasingly replaced by beaten earth. Subsistence had priority over mobility within the city: the centres of the Roman *insulae* were cleared for cultivation and some new houses were built further into the width of the streets. This new pattern of domestic house-building – facing on to the street and with a large garden behind – anticipates a type that remains common in the Veneto even today.

Although San Zeno notes in a sermon that a large church was built by his order, no Christian church of that early date has yet been discovered. Two Christian basilicas, with fourth-century mosaic floors, have been identified below the cathedral complex. But the most complete, and suggestive, of the early churches is Santo Stefano, which was founded in the early fifth century and may have served as the first cathedral. Theoderic, at the end of his reign, demonstrated his hatred for Catholicism by destroying the first building. It was soon rebuilt, and the new church may well have been all the more conscientiously preserved in compensation for the Ostrogoth's intemperate sacrilege.

The people of Verona never forgot or forgave his evil action. When as an emerging free commune they built the most beautiful of all Italian Romanesque churches and dedicated it to San Zeno, Theoderic was commemorated on its façade by a carving that shows him rise from his bath, mount his horse and, followed by his dogs, hunt a deer; but the deer flees further and further ahead, and finally leads him to hell.

The Piazza delle Erbe, on the site of the Roman Forum, has always been Verona's main market square. The narrowest houses around its perimeter are the bases of early medieval defence towers. By the twelfth century the skyline of Verona bristled with about seventy of these family towers.

2 The Late Middle Ages: The Commune and the Scaligers

There is no world without Verona's walls,
But purgatory, torture, hell itself.
Hence-banished is banish'd from the world,
And world's exile is death.

Shakespeare, *Romeo and Juliet*

In a world where a man was defined more by the town he belonged to than by his class or social level, identification with one's town reached a pitch unknown elsewhere, and no condition seemed worse than that of the bandit and the exile, the man who had no homeland and no roots.

Giuliano Procacci, *History of the Italian People*,
'The Years around 1000'

In the early twelfth century Verona became a self-governing commune. The polychrome bas-relief in the lunette over the main entrance to the church of San Zeno celebrates the foundation of the commune under the protection of San Zeno, who holds the standard of the city and tramples on the devil. The people, portrayed as foot soldiers, are on his left; the nobility, represented as cavalry, are on his right. The band of carvings above the lunette bears the signature of the sculptor, Nicolò. Some of the miracles performed by San Zeno are depicted on the band below.

In the years around the millennium north Italian towns, well ahead of the rest of Europe, began to function as independent urban centres where goods, services and ideas were exchanged for the mutual benefit of all social classes. The old rigid feudal hierarchies were gradually replaced by new contractual associations between landlords and peasants. The middle classes formed organizations which gave them a political voice. The absolute authority of the Holy Roman Emperors was called into question by more sophisticated societies that yearned for civic autonomy.

Verona was politically, culturally and economically precocious even by Italian standards. Its lower classes had formed unofficial organizations even in the days of Charlemagne. Intellectual freedom had been less rigidly circumscribed by the Church than elsewhere. Verona was one of the few medieval cities where the monks had continued to transcribe heretical 'pagan' texts, and its cathedral library had the richest collection of codices in north Italy. In the tenth century the city was served by more tailors, bakers, millers, hosiers and smiths than Florence could boast two centuries later.

By the end of the eleventh century contemporary chroniclers cease to mention Imperial or feudal titles when writing about Verona; from now on the people are referred to as *cittadini* – citizens. In 1107 Verona was rich enough to make a commercial treaty, on equal terms, with Venice. In 1119 its army was powerful enough to come to the aid of Milan which was engaged in a prolonged war with Como. In the documents that relate these events Verona is no longer a 'county' of the Holy Roman Emperor. It is called a city or district. The names of the first consuls are recorded in 1136. Verona had become a self-governing commune.

The birth of the commune is announced on the façade of the church of San Zeno, which was enlarged at the city's expense by 1138. The polychrome bas-relief over the main doors portrays San Zeno, patron saint of the commune, under whose protection the two social groups – the people, portrayed as foot soldiers, on his left; the nobility, shown as cavalry, on his right – are united. He is trampling on a devil, which may represent corrupt practices by Church authorities, such as the buying and selling of Church preferments. It is an unusually early and specific iconographic commemoration of the foundation of an Italian commune; and it serves as a reminder that the new style of government was not the result of a popular revolution. Nor was it a representative democracy in the modern sense but rather an alliance between the upper and lower orders.

It is not by accident that the citizens of the new commune were portrayed as militia in the San Zeno lunette. Independence had to be fought for. The Hohenstaufen Frederick I, who was elected Emperor in 1152, challenged the sovereign rights of the newly formed communes, which drew together in a league, usually but not always supported by the Papacy. After a succession of squabbles and battles a compromise was achieved towards the end of the century: the communes would retain their civic autonomy while recognizing the over-all sovereignty of the Emperor.

The struggle, which involved the whole of Italy, was the origin of the continuing and ever-more complex conflicts between Guelfs (supporters of the Pope and the independent communes) and Ghibellines (those who favoured the Empire) – and the numerous factions that soon developed within those two parties. The tale of Romeo and Juliet is set against the factional strife which was particularly acute in Verona,

The bronze doors of San Zeno consist of 48 panels depicting scenes from the Old and New Testaments, from the life of San Zeno and allegorical and biblical figures. They were made by three separate masters in the twelfth century. The oldest panels are those on the left door, shown here.

The wooden 'ship's keel' ceiling of the church of San Zeno is an early example of a ceiling type seen only in the Veneto.

which became the leading Ghibelline power and the route through which the German Emperors hoped to establish rule over Italy. The tragedy of the star-crossed lovers was originally written in the sixteenth century by Luigi da Porto, a native of the neighbouring city of Vicenza. The story itself has no historic basis. But there was a family called Montecchi (Montague). The remains of their castle stand above the village of Montecchio Maggiore on the road between Vicenza and Verona. They were allies of Ezzelino III da Romano, and as such played a role in the downfall of the commune of Verona.

Ezzelino was the most insanely inspired thug in a succession of vicious tyrants who took advantage of the chronic political instability of the communal governments. John Addington Symonds has described him thus: 'Ezzelino, a small, pale, wiry man, with terror in his face and enthusiasm for evil in his heart, lived a foe to luxury, cold to the pathos of children, dead to the enchantment of women. His one passion was the greed of power, heightened by the lust for blood.'

The political career of this repellent personality opened in the 1220s when he was appointed chief justice of Verona. In 1232 he switched his allegiance from the Guelf to the Ghibelline party, opened the gates of north Italy to the Emperor Frederick II, and became the henchman of that subtle and ambitious ruler. Ezzelino went on to conquer a string of cities – including Vicenza, Padua and Treviso – which he ruled, from Verona, as an absolute dictator. His gratuitous torturings, bloody campaigns, sackings and devastations of the countryside continued even after the death of Frederick in 1254 and finally alienated a group of former supporters. He died in 1259, 'in silence like a boar at bay, rending from his wounds the dressings that his foes had placed to keep him alive,' according to Symonds. Dante condemned him to the seventh circle of the *Inferno*, where he will drown forever in a river of boiling blood.

The Communal Cityscape

In the years between the foundation of the commune and the unlamented death of its destroyer Verona had expanded rapidly. As the centre was repopulated by waves of migration from the countryside, land-values soared and programmes of urban improvement, such as the cutting of the Adigetto Canal between the two legs of the Adige, were initiated. A dense forest of defence towers sprouted from the fortified

The Romanesque façade of the Cathedral was modified in the fifteenth century when the large Gothic mullioned windows were opened up. Its portico, supported by columns resting on stone lions, was built under the commune at about the same time as that of San Zeno. The relief carvings are by Nicolò, the same master who worked on San Zeno. On either side of the porch, Old Testament prophets are shown into the church by two of Charlemagne's paladins.

palaces of family clans. There were about seventy such tower-houses in the town (the Ezzelino palace was on the site of Palazzo Emilei).

Meetings of the council were held in private houses until the end of the twelfth century, when the councillors built one of the first palaces in Italy specifically intended to house local government offices. It incorporated the tower of the Lamberti family which had been raised in 1172 in what was then an isolated part of the city where no development had taken place since the area was flattened by fire in the seventh century. The base is constructed in alternate courses of brick and ivory limestone – a decorative surface typical of the local Romanesque style, and which indicates that the family was concerned with aesthetic effect as well as self-defence. The communal government headquarters, completed in 1196, was constructed around the rectangular courtyard that preserves the original brickwork, striped like that of the tower base and pierced by triforate windows. The sturdy round-headed archways supported on rusticated pillars and the frieze of tiny Romanesque arches under the roofline are also original.

The urban panorama was otherwise dominated by churches, whose architecture and sculptural decorations reflect the cosmopolitan atmosphere of communal Verona. Some – San Lorenzo, Santi Apostoli and the lower church of San Fermo – were founded by transalpine religious orders and follow the plan of earlier French or Norman churches; others, built a little later, show the influence of Emilian or Lombard models. But although not architecturally innovative these buildings have an immense charm that derives from the happy use of materials – pink bricks combined with rosy local marble or with the ochre and ivory of tufo.

The two most important churches were San Zeno and the cathedral, which was enlarged after 1139, a little later than San Zeno. The relief carvings on both façades are mainly by the same master, Nicolò, who also worked on the cathedral of Ferrara. Their subject-matter is a peculiar mixture of sacred and profane – legends associated with Verona's past and episodes from chivalrous poems of the period as well as scenes from the Old and New Testaments – which indicates that local history and contemporary literature played at least as important a role in the spiritual life of communal Verona as the Bible. On the porch of the cathedral Old Testament prophets are shown into the church by two of Charlemagne's paladins, Orlando on the left, Oliviero on the

The Torre dei Lamberti is the oldest and tallest tower in Verona. It was originally built in 1172 by the Lamberti family as the defence tower of their palace. Twenty-four years later the young communal government took it over and used it as the tower of their first purpose-built headquarters. It is seen here from the courtyard of the communal palace. The tower was raised above its Romanesque base in the fifteenth century at about the same time that the external staircase was applied to the courtyard. The striped brickwork of the walls of the courtyard and base of the tower was typical of Romanesque buildings in Verona.

right. The iconography of San Zeno's porch, as we have seen, is concerned with the foundation of the commune, with San Zeno's miracles and with the baleful Theoderic's fateful deer-hunt. The main doors of San Zeno consist of forty-eight panels – the subjects here are mainly religious – worked in bronze by three separate masters before and after an earthquake which erupted in 1117 and delayed the completion of the new church.

These are today among the most admired Romanesque doors in Italy, and so popular with tourists that they have to be protected from the crowds by barriers. It is all the more worth remembering, then, that the cult art of one period is sometimes the bane of another. The French traveller Hippolyte Taine wrote in 1865 that he had 'seen nothing so barbaric except in Pisa. The Christ at the pillar looks like a bear climbing a tree . . . The Christ on the throne has no skull, the entire face being absorbed by the chin, the wild and protruding eyes are like those of a frog, while the winged angels are like human bats.'

Whatever one's reaction to its bronze doors, San Zeno is an irresistible building. There is an endearing innocence about its creamy stone slope-shouldered façade, flanked on one side by the four-square brick tower of an earlier monastery and on the other by the slender bell-tower with its zipper of red bricks and conical hat. But the interior, with its spacious central nave lit by the huge circular wheel of fortune that pierces the façade, has a confident grandeur unmatched by any other church interior in the city. The coffered wooden 'ship's keel' ceiling is a type seen only in the Veneto, but the commanding row of statues of Christ and the Apostles on the balustrade over the entrance to the crypt have a Germanic Gothic sway that announces the early arrival of a new style in Verona.

For the young communal government, which met here to celebrate solemn secular as well as religious occasions, San Zeno was the pivot of civic pride. Every north Italian town has a building that sums up the meaning of the word *campanilismo*, excessive attachment to everything within sight of one's native bell-tower. For Verona, that building is San Zeno. The cathedral was later extensively modified: only the porch, the baptistery and parts of the apse survive from the Romanesque building. But no subsequent government, however despotic or careless, dared to tamper with the architecture of this monument to communal self-definition.

The octagonal brick tambour of the church of Santo Stefano was built by Lombard architects when the church, one of the oldest in Verona, was enlarged in the twelfth century.

In the 1450s Mantegna's *San Zeno Madonna* was placed in the apse over the high altar. It was the first Renaissance painting seen in Verona, and the first Italian *sacra conversazione* in which the figures are set in realistic space. The Madonna's halo, and the base of her throne, echo the wheel-of-fortune window at the far end of the church.

The most architecturally complex of the churches enlarged under the commune is Santo Stefano. Its octagonal brick tambour, built by Lombard architects, and the double ambulatory of the interior apse are unique in Verona. The façade, also rebuilt in the twelfth century, was used as an informal register of noteworthy events, such as floods and the collapse of bridges, which are recorded by inscriptions. One of them concerns a visit by Frederick II who spent a month in Verona in 1245. His entourage included a private zoo consisting of one elephant, twenty-four camels and five lions. The elephant was the star attraction.

Frederick II was not merely a remarkable man. He was, deservedly it seems, known in his lifetime as Stupor Mundi. He was an ambitious ruler, but also a scholar and polylinguist, exactly the sort of cultivated and worldly intellectual the bookish Veronesi were likely to respect. He adored Italy and was better equipped to understand it than any other German Emperor before or after. His efforts to create a united German-Italian state were ultimately unsuccessful. But during the turbulent years when, thanks to Ezzelino, the transalpine connection was re-established, Verona was irradiated by northern chivalrous culture earlier and more lastingly than any other city in the Veneto.

The Scaliger Dynasty

And then come the festas. Oh, heavens above,
Those blondes causing fervours and torments of love!
Girls, still more girls come to join in the rout,
To flirt or to scamper or wander about
With a 'yes?' or 'why not?' or 'a word in your ear;
I'm off for a while but I'll soon be back here.'

There are barons and marquesses here to be found,
Civil and gracious, from all lands around:
From Flanders and Germany, Spain, and still more:
Both from Italy's regions and England's far shore.

The streets are a-buzz as Theology blames
Philosophers' doubts and astrologers' claims.

> A poem written by Manoello Giudeo, *c.* 1320, in honour of Cangrande Della Scala

Even as the queen of the south sought Jerusalem or as Pallas sought Helicon, so did I seek Verona, to scrutinise by the faithful testimony of my own eyes the things which I had heard. And there I beheld your splendour, I beheld and at the same time handled your bounty; and even as I had formerly suspected excess on the side of the reports, so did I afterwards recognise that it was the facts themselves that exceeded.

> Dante Alighieri, *Epistola* X, in which he dedicates the *Paradiso* to Cangrande Della Scala

Ezzelino's reign of terror extinguished the proud spirit of the commune in Verona. Although he had never been properly elected as leader of the city, the commune, and particularly the lower middle classes, had

Above The equestrian monument of Cangrande's nephew Mastino II Della Scala crowns his mausoleum in the Scaliger burial ground. The statue may be by the same sculptor who made Cangrande's more compelling monument.

Below The equestrian monument of Cangrande Della Scala, the greatest of the Scaliger *signori*, was made by an unknown artist in the 1350s, more than twenty years after Cangrande's death. Despite an insensitive restoration in the late nineteenth century it remains the most artistically powerful post-classical equestrian statue before Donatello's Gattamelata monument in Padua. It originally stood with the other Scaliger monuments in their burial ground, the Arche Scaligeri. It is now dramatically sited on a bridge in the Castelvecchio Museum.

Far right The stylistically unwieldy mausoleum of Cansignorio Della Scala was completed in 1375, twelve years before the Della Scala dynasty lost control of Verona. The inert stone Cansignorio on horseback communicates none of the poetry and grace of the Cangrande, made only twenty-five years earlier. It is signed by Bonino da Campione, who also worked for the Visconti, rulers of Verona after the Scaligers.

condoned his regime. The liberties that had licensed such atrocities were suspect. The institutions of communal government were retained, but a new style of leadership was wanted.

From shortly after Ezzelino's death until towards the close of the fourteenth century Verona was ruled by successive members of one family, the Della Scala, or Scaliger, dynasty. They were not monarchs, in the sense that they never claimed a divine right of heredity. The institutions of communal government, including the Great Council of 500 members, remained more or less intact and, at least at the start, went through the motions of 'electing' them as leaders.

The institutionalization of effective political leadership under a dynastic *signoria* was a compromise solution adopted by many Italian communes. Since this institution was peculiar to medieval Italy the Italian title *signore* (singular), *signori* (plural) is used here. The Scaliger became the most powerful *signori* in north Italy. They continued the Ghibelline policies of Ezzelino, and were eventually made Imperial vicars by Henry VII. They married into the leading Italian princely families, the Este, Visconti and Carrara; and their court was a magnet for the greatest artists and intellectuals of the day. Giotto, Petrarch and Boccaccio all paid them tribute. Dante, a Ghibelline in exile from his native Guelf Florence, was particularly appreciative of their hospitality and their political allegiance to the German Empire. He saw Verona as the great hope for peace and the Imperial cause: Henry VII and Cangrande Della Scala were his 'lights of the world'. His writing is full of references to the Della Scala, Verona and its territory; it is one of the very few Italian cities about which he never complains. His eldest son Pietro settled in the city, became a judge, and the direct line of the family continued until the sixteenth century.

The Scaliger eventually conquered a string of important Italian cities in the Veneto, Lombardy and across the Apennines as far south as Lucca, thus challenging the balance of power which was beginning to weigh in favour of Florence and Venice. Historians have suggested that if the greatest of the Della Scala, Cangrande, had not died young and if his successors had not been relatively weak personalities, the emerging power of the Italian city-states might have been checked, at least for a time, and the history of Italy might have taken a different course.

The origins of the Della Scala are obscure. Patricians of that name had been martyred during Ezzelino's reign of terror. But it seems

The Piazza dei Signori is so-called after the Scaliger *signori* or lords who ruled Verona from 1262 to 1387 and made this part of the city their political and residential headquarters. The most beautiful building in the piazza, however, is the arcaded Loggia del Consiglio (on the left of the photograph) which was completed in the 1490s – more than a century after the Scaligers had left the city – to house the offices of the local government. Its open design emphasized the transferral of power from the tyrannical *signori* to a publicly accountable and stable government. The building at the head of the piazza was the private residence of Cangrande Della Scala who entertained Dante, Giotto and Boccaccio here. But it has unfortunately suffered from many crude restorations.

Left The Torre del Gardello, which rises above the south-west corner of the main market square, Piazza delle Erbe, was Verona's first public clock tower. It was built in the 1370s by the tyrannical ruler Cansignorio Della Scala, who had a passion for building and hoped to appease the merchants on whom the wealth of the city depended by improving their amenities. The winged lion of St Mark below is one of many lions erected in Verona during the four centuries of Venetian dominion. The façade of Palazzo Maffei, behind the lion, is one of Verona's most prominent and handsome Baroque palaces.

Right The arcaded Casa dei Mercanti in Piazza delle Erbe was built in the early fourteenth century as the merchants' headquarters. Verona has always been one of the richest mercantile cities in Italy.

unlikely that members of an established family could have risen so fast within the communal government, especially as Ezzelino had himself been a patrician. New men were wanted to cleanse the air that was still rancid with the blood he had shed. One theory has it that the Della Scala were artisans who took their name from a family business manufacturing staircases (*scala* means 'staircase' or 'ladder').

Mastino Della Scala was elected *capitano* of the communal government, by the unanimous will of the people, in 1262. In 1277 he was assassinated by enemies and succeeded by his brother Alberto. Alberto was appointed *capitano* for life, but he behaved more like a prince. He changed the government statutes, introducing a requirement that elections could not take place without his consent; he destroyed the defence towers of rival families and forbade the building of private castles or towers in Verona or in the district. Alberto's son Bartolomeo was *signore* only from 1302 until his early and much-lamented death two years later. He was popular and conscientious, but is most famous today for having been the first Della Scala to receive Dante – and for the tale of Romeo and Juliet, which was specifically set by its original author during his short rule. Bartolomeo's brother Alboino, by contrast, was a true despot. He established total authority by taking control of the merchant and artisan guilds, on which the economy depended and which had so far enjoyed a good measure of privilege and freedom under the Della Scala, as well as of government. Dante detested him and called him the vilest of men.

In 1308 Alboino was joined as *signore* by his younger brother, Cangrande, who assumed full control three years later at the age of only 20. Cangrande enhanced the prestige of the Scaliger *signoria* by creating one of the most splendid Gothic courts in Europe. Like Frederick II, to whom Boccaccio compared him, Cangrande was one of those larger-than-life figures who seem too amazing to be true and whose popular reputation scrupulous modern historians try to deflate. And yet nobody who knew or observed him ever denied that he was a ruthlessly courageous warrior but magnanimous in victory, a shrewd and tireless statesman, as well as a cultivated intellectual who understood the work of the artists and writers with whom he surrounded himself when at court. Dante, who called him his 'beloved greyhound' (Cangrande means 'big dog'), had reason to be grateful to him, but would perhaps not have shown such real affection if he hadn't also admired his patron's grasp of literature.

Cangrande died in 1329 after a successful siege of Treviso. His body was carried back to Verona in state and entombed over the door of the court chapel. The tomb was opened in 1921 on the occasion of the sixth centenary of Dante's death and his sword removed to the Castelvecchio Museum. His equestrian monument, sculpted in the 1350s (also now in the Museum), shows a boyish figure on horseback with his tournament helm thrown back to reveal an enigmatic Gothic smile. It is the most powerfully suggestive post-classical equestrian statue before Donatello's Gattamelata monument in Padua. But the artist remains anonymous, and it does not reveal much about Cangrande's personality. Perhaps if the portrait Giotto is said to have painted of him had survived, we would know more about what he was like.

The Scaligers never produced another leader of Cangrande's stature, and their domain was gradually whittled away as successive weak and grasping members of the family wasted energy on dynastic squabbles. A turning point in foreign affairs came in 1336 when Florence and Venice formed an alliance against Verona. Florence badly wanted to retrieve Lucca; and Venice resented Verona's appropriation of the shallow waters of the southern Po delta where salt was cheaply evaporated and

Right The portal of the Gothic upper church of San Fermo with a statue of St Francis in the lunette above the door. The Franciscan church stands at the opposite side of the city from the Dominican Sant'Anastasia.

Far right The wooden 'ship's keel' ceiling of the upper church of San Fermo is a later and more elaborate version of the type in San Zeno. It runs the entire length of the church and the shape of its profile determines the outline of the triumphal arch in the apse.

extracted. Then Venice took Treviso, its first foothold on the mainland. Cangrande's nephew, Mastino II, hadn't the nerve or the wit to retaliate effectively.

By 1348 the Scaligers were reduced to a small, if still brilliant, *signoria*. That was the year the great plague struck Europe. The population of Verona, reduced to about 20 000, did not recover until the middle of the next century. And the disaster was compounded for Verona by an earthquake and an invasion of locusts which destroyed crops. Petrarch, who was in Verona that spring, had an inauspicious dream announcing the death of Laura, the mistress of his love poetry. In a letter written in 1350 Petrarch describes a journey he made from France into Italy with the entourage of a French Bishop. They stopped to rest on a grassy hill above Lake Garda: 'On the right were the Alps, capped with snow in mid-summer, and the surface of the deep lake whipped up by a breeze into little waves like the sea. Ahead and behind us were small radiant hills; to the left a vast, spacious, intensely fertile green plain on which it pleased us to gaze for a long time.' The Bishop, 'speaking in a loud voice so that everyone could hear said: "I have to confess that your country is much better than ours, and much more beautiful." ' Then, seeing that the Italian poet was pleased with this compliment, he added: ' "But our state is more tranquil, and our government more tolerant than yours." '

Cangrande II, a paranoic tyrant nicknamed 'Mad Dog' by his people, succeeded his weak father Mastino II in 1352 and ruled until he was murdered in 1359 by his brother Cansignorio. Cansignorio retained power by killing off more popular relatives, imprisoning the natural sons of Cangrande II, and by hanging or decapitating former political allies who threatened his position. He died in 1375 at the age of 36.

Verona was still an immensely rich mercantile city, its principal activity being the manufacture of wool cloth, of which it was one of the major Italian suppliers. Nevertheless, surrounded as they were by the stronger powers, the Scaligers' foreign policy was reduced to a twisting and turning in search of protection through alliances – now with the Visconti of Milan, now with Venice. In 1385 Gian Galeazzo Visconti became ruler of Milan. He was young, active, shrewd, ambitious and unscrupulous. One by one the trusted friends of the Scaligers abandoned the dying *signoria* to go into the service of Gian Galeazzo, who formed an alliance with the Carrara of Padua and, on the night of 18 October 1387, forced the surrender of Verona.

It wasn't quite the end. Although the people of Verona had come to detest the despotic and decadent Scaligers, they resented foreign rule even more. In 1390 they rose up and expelled the Visconti's representatives, who returned only after sacking the city – breaching the walls they had themselves rebuilt to defend it – for three days. The Veronesi fought this futile revolution bravely, although they must have known that their days as an independent power were numbered.

Above The church and bell tower of Sant'Anastasia seen from the Torre dei Lamberti. Sant'Anastasia was completed in the early fifteenth century according to the original fourteenth-century plans. The bell tower, the second tallest of Verona's towers after the Torre dei Lamberti, was erected in the 1460s.

Below The city of the princess, one of the surviving fragments of Pisanello's fresco of the Legend of St George and the Princess, was painted for the Pellegrini chapel of Sant' Anastasia in 1438. The architecture of the princess's city echoes that of Scaliger Verona. Photograph: Scala/Art Resource, New York.

SANTVS·GIORGIVS·

After Gian Galeazzo died in 1402 Verona was ruled for a few years by the Carrara *signoria*. But Gian Galeazzo's death had left the field open to Venice. Having consolidated its maritime trade routes, the Most Serene Republic now wanted to create a toll-free passage across the mainland to the Alpine passes. Although the exiled Scaligers and their Imperial allies continued to plot for a return to power, their aristocratic supporters in Verona were divided and enfeebled. They were certainly no match for the richest state in north Italy, and the only one with a stable government.

Verona under the Scaligers

It was under the Scaligers that the Verona we recognize today began to take shape. Cangrande's walls, built in 1325, extended the city very nearly to its present limits. And as it expanded squadrons of painters and sculptors – from Emilia-Romagna, Tuscany, Venice and Lombardy as well as native artists – were employed to decorate the new palaces and churches. The 'new' Gothic art and architecture, of which Verona was a north Italian capital, flourished under the Della Scala as magnificently as in Bohemia or Burgundy.

The Scaliger power centre was concentrated in and around the piazza still known as 'dei Signori'. The individual Scaliger palaces were linked by an uninterrupted series of arcaded courtyards paved in herring-bone brick and extending as far as the eastern branch of the Adige where the modern post office stands in the forlorn nineteenth-century Piazza Indipendenza. The palace where Cangrande received Dante is now the prefecturate; Cansignorio's inner-city fortress palace, built in the 1360s, is the tribunal. Both these buildings have been so frequently adapted for the administrative use of later governments, and so mutilated by well-intentioned restorations, that it is impossible to reconstruct their original appearance.

It is the graveyard where they lie buried outside the court chapel, Santa Maria Antica, rather than the palaces where they lived that evokes the aesthetic ideal of the Scaliger court as it evolved during their rule. The Arche Scaligeri, as this extraordinary complex of tombs and funerary architecture is known, is the most complete and exquisitely concentrated memorial to any Italian *signoria* and an epitome of northern European chivalric culture. It stands between the two

Above The fourteenth-century portal of Sant'Anastasia was the only part of the façade to be completed. The highly decorative use of polychrome marbles is typical of the sensuous appreciation of the colour and texture of stone from the local quarries that enlivens so many of Verona's buildings. The carvings are in a neo-Romanesque style that harks back to the example of the master of the San Zeno and Cathedral doors.

Below The vaulted and frescoed ceiling of the nave of Sant'Anastasia is supported on ogival arches borne by twelve massive columns of red Verona marble.

surviving Scaliger palaces, enclosed by a flexible iron grille, the geometric quattrofoil design of which is elaborated with the miniature ladders that were the canting emblem of the dynasty.

The more despotic their rule, the more lavishly the Scaligers commemorated their deaths. The tomb of Mastino I, the first member of the family to head the communal government, is completely plain. That of Alberto I is decorated with relief carvings on all four sides. The imagery on Cangrande's sarcophagus mixes religious subjects with celebrations of his conquests. His smiling effigy was probably carved in the year after his death by a sculptor whose nationality has never been identified. Scholars have tried to relate it to French, German and Sienese examples, but there seems to be nothing quite like it anywhere, apart from the figure of San Zeno laughing in the church of San Zeno. The tomb of his nephew Mastino II, who had no conquests to celebrate, is decorated, in a more considered and polished style than Cangrande's, with religious subjects only.

From the pinnacles of their spired mausoleums the equestrian statues of Mastino II and his son Cansignorio appear to be engaged in a perpetual aerial jousting tournament. Both commissioned their own monuments and watched them being built from the windows of their palaces. The Mastino tabernacle, completed in the 1350s by an unknown master, is architecturally more restrained, the most beautiful sections being the sculptures of Old Testament subjects in the tympana. The crowning statue of Mastino on horseback may be by the same sculptor who made the more compelling equestrian statue of Cangrande. Cansignorio's mausoleum was completed by 1375. With its thickets of cusps, spires and pointed arches sprouting from twisted stump-like columns, the architectural ensemble has an egregiously unwieldy quality that may remind some modern visitors of the Victoria and Albert Memorial in London. The stone Cansignorio on horseback communicates none of the poetry and grace of the Cangrande, made only some twenty-five years earlier. It is signed by the Lombard sculptor Bonino da Campione, who also worked for the Visconti in Milan.

Cansignorio is reputed to have said that if he had been born as an ordinary citizen he would have sacrificed all other pleasures and duties for the pleasure of building. He spent large sums of his personal fortune on improving the city's amenities, which he hoped would impress and

Above The swallow-tail, or 'Ghibelline', battlements of the massive red-brick Castelvecchio and two of the castle's seven guard towers. The Castelvecchio was built between 1355 and 1375 by the tyrannical Cangrande II and Cansignorio Della Scala as a fortress against their increasingly restive subjects. The Castelvecchio now houses a superb museum and art gallery.

Below A section of the city wall built by the communal government in the twelfth century was used to separate the two sections of the fourteenth-century Castelvecchio: the *reggia*, or residential palace, on the outer side; the *caserma*, or barracks, on the city side.

earn the gratitude of his subjects, and particularly of the all-important merchants. It was during his otherwise decadent rule that Verona became known as *marmorea*, the marble city.

The most important market square was the Piazza Maggiore, now the Piazza delle Erbe. The merchants' headquarters, the arcaded Casa dei Mercanti, was erected there in the early fourteenth century. In the 1370s Cansignorio contributed the city's first public clock tower, the Torre del Gardello, and resurrected a Roman basin and statue (now known as 'Madonna Verona') to create the central fountain, to which drinking water was piped from a spring near the city.

The Piazza Maggiore was only the largest of the public spaces that served as markets. Even the courtyard of the communal palace was rented out to shopkeepers, and has been confusingly known ever since as the Cortile del Mercato Vecchio. Each market square was equipped with a stone or brass measuring standard for cloth and, often, a devotional image housed in one of the little Gothic aedicules supported on slender columns that you still see in Verona (although most are now reproductions) and that are known locally as *capitelli*.

The two poles of religious life were the Dominican church of Sant'Anastasia and the Franciscan San Fermo, which stand on either side of the political centre. Their enlargement was largely financed by Gugliemo da Castelbarco, whose tomb above the cemetery gate of Sant'Anastasia Ruskin, in one of his frenzies of admiration for Verona, was to describe as 'the most perfect Gothic sepulchral monument in the world'. The façade of Sant'Anastasia was never completed beyond its polychrome marble portal, decorated with neo-Romanesque bas-reliefs that may have been carved by the same sculptor who made the effigy of the scholar and astronomer Antonio Pelicani in San Fermo.

The Gothic church of San Fermo was built on top of the earlier Romanesque church, resulting in a double-decker building of which the earlier, lower part is now partly submerged below ground level, which has subsequently risen by several metres. The most striking and original architectural feature of the interior of the Gothic upper church is the coffered and polylobed wooden ceiling, a more elaborate version of the ship's keel ceiling in San Zeno. It is perhaps the most magnificent example of this ceiling type in the Veneto, and it runs down the whole of the nave, its outline determining that of the triumphal arch in the apse. Ruskin drew and described the particular shape of the arches on

The three-span bridge of the Castelvecchio offered the Scaligers an escape route northwards towards Germany and their Imperial allies. The size of the largest span was calculated to allow trading vessels to pass through it on their way to and from the docks in the city centre. Like all of Verona's bridges this is a faithful reconstruction of the original which was demolished in the Second World War.

the Gothic façade of this marvellous church. 'This arch, together with the rest of the arcade, is wrought in fine stone with a band of inlaid red brick, the whole chiselled and fitted with exquisite precision, all Venetian work being coarse in comparison. Throughout the streets of Verona, arches and windows of the thirteenth century are of continual occurrence, wrought, in this manner, with brick and stone; sometimes the brick alternating with the stones of the arch.' This particular ogival shape continued to be used in Verona until well into the Renaissance.

No ecclesiastic or civic building looms as large in Verona as the massive red-brick Castelvecchio, with its seven guard towers and swallow-tail battlements. It was built between 1355 and 1375 by Cangrande II and Cansignorio as a refuge from the subject citizens whom they had more reason to fear than foreign invasion; and it had all the traditional features of a pre-communal feudal castle: residential apartments with rooms for holding court, a chapel, guard walkways, a moat and drawbridges. A stretch of the old communal wall, further strengthened by a moat, was used to divide its two sections: the barracks (*caserma*) on the city side; the residential palace (*reggia*) on the – safer – outer side.

It stood in what was then an isolated edge of the city, with its three-span bridge, fortified by battlements and turrets, providing an escape route northwards across the Adige towards Imperial Germany. But even then commercial considerations were not neglected: the size of the largest span nearest the right bank of the river was calculated to admit trading vessels on their way to and from the docks in the city centre. The Castelvecchio became the 'old' castle shortly after it was completed

A section of the Mura dei Visconti, the walls built by the Visconti after they took control of Verona in 1387. After the Visconti built three new fortresses the Castelvecchio became known as the old (*vecchio*) castle. The southern entrance to Piazza Brà from Corso Porta Nuova is through two arches built in 1389 to support a stretch of the raised covered passage that linked the Castelvecchio to the Visconti citadel on the south-east of the Piazza.

when the Visconti occupied it and refortified the city with three new castles. A stretch of the raised walkway they built between the Scaliger castle and their own inner-city citadel still runs above the gateway to Piazza Brà.

Even a brief architectural tour of the Scaligers' Verona should include the frescoed portraits of the city by Altichiero Altichieri and Pisanello, the two greatest of the painters born in fourteenth-century Verona. Both are in the church of Sant'Anastasia. Altichiero's fresco in the Cavalli chapel, although painted in the 1380s when the Scaliger regime was on the verge of collapse, is a faithful recreation of the city as it might have looked in the days of Mastino II. The airy, fully articulated buildings are so realistic that they give the impression not of painted architecture but of architecture rebuilt in paint; and they did in fact influence the style of subsequent building in the city.

In the city of the princess in Pisanello's famous fresco of the Legend of St George, French castle architecture is fused with elements of Cansignorio's marble city – the quattolobe of the Arche ironwork, the cusps of his mausoleum, the battlements of the Castelvecchio walls and bridge – to create one of the most poetic images of Gothic civilization (and the inspiration for countless productions of *Romeo and Juliet*).

Pisanello's enchanted city has been aptly described as a 'lucid delirium'. When it was painted in 1438 the Scaligers were in exile in Germany and their palaces had been occupied by Venetian officials for more than three decades. Impotent and impoverished, Verona clung to the aesthetic ideals of a glorious past that was just within living memory. It resisted the precepts of the new classical Renaissance art that was percolating into north Italy from Tuscany and remained the last centre in the Veneto of the International Gothic style. And just as the real marble city of the Scaligers was beginning to decay and lose its purpose its essence was preserved in paint by that style's last and greatest master.

3 Renaissance Verona

1405–1509

> Noble Verona! to climate, river, site,
> Are added wonders: palace and tower of might,
> Piazza, loggias, churches, bridges fair
> The Arche di Signori, fountains clear.
>
> Anonymous poem written at the end of the fifteenth century

In June 1405 the exhausted city yielded to the inevitable. The Venetian army stood outside the city walls. Its representatives were received in the Piazza delle Erbe with a nicely turned Latin oration. In July the Bolla d'oro, the Golden Bull according to which Verona was to be governed, was ratified in Venice by Doge Michele Steno. He welcomed the subject city with the words of Isaiah, 'The people that walked in darkness have seen a great light', thus emphasizing that Verona had not been conquered by force, but had voluntarily ceded its autonomy. Verona remained a Venetian subject until the collapse of the Republic nearly four centuries later.

Venice guaranteed that the statutes of the commune and the merchants' guilds would be revived and respected. The highest government offices, however, were filled by Venetian patricians who served as rectors for not more than two years at a time. The Venetian *podestà*, or chief justice, had full powers over the maintenance of law and order; the *capitano* was both military commander and fiscal officer. The communal government, which remained responsible for municipal administration, was lead by an executive council of twelve men, the Consiglio dei Dodici, which elected a sub-council, the Consiglio Grande, of fifty members chosen from a social and economic cross-section of citizens who served for six months at a time.

In the first years of its dominion Venice was engaged in a territorial war with Filippo Maria Visconti, and had no wish to alienate the subject city that was the key to the expansion of its mainland empire beyond the Adige and Mincio rivers. Venice needed local loyalty and expertise. Although a large contingent of infantry was installed in the old Visconti citadel, care was taken not to disrupt traditional privileges and habits either in Verona itself or in the country villages. Nevertheless, relations between the two cities were at first strained. The wool industry was allowed to run down. Crops in the fertile plain to the

Reading about recent history at a convenient spot outside the fifteenth-century Loggia del Consiglio.

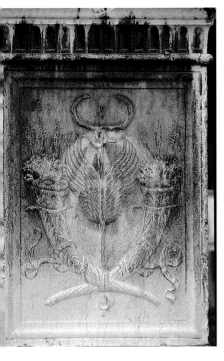

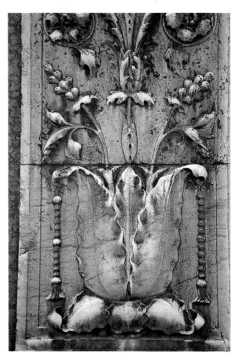

he Loggia del Consiglio was
ompleted in 1492 to house the
nlarged local government. Its arcaded
round floor opening directly on to
iazza dei Signori was intended to
emonstrate that Verona was now
overned by a stable representative
ouncil that had no fear of attack from
s citizens. Although the Loggia is the
ost architecturally distinguished
uilding raised in the first century of
enetian rule, its architect, if there was

one, is unknown. The row of statues
on the roofline represent famous native
Romans. Verona was intensely proud
of its Roman origins which gave the
city cultural superiority over its
Venetian masters. But only one of the
Romans, Catullus, is now thought to
have been born in or near Verona. The
rich and delicate carvings on the façade
were executed by Lombard
stonemasons, who were in plentiful
supply in Renaissance Verona.

south of Verona, which was one of the main theatres of the war with the Visconti, were trampled by armies. Whole villages were depopulated, the soil went uncultivated. There were occasional riots when the people gathered on one of the bridges and cried out for the Della Scala and the German Empire, of which the city was still, nominally, a vicarate.

Venice considered tightening control over the local government. After some debate it opted instead for a policy of encouraging civic self-definition. In 1450 the statutes of the Bolla d'oro were revised, after which they remained substantially unchanged throughout the period of Venetian dominion. The Consiglio Grande was enlarged to 122 members. Gradually the lower social orders were excluded from government office, as they had been in Venice. In compensation Venice undertook to improve public hygiene, and built a new slaughterhouse and fish market. Newly appointed Venetian officials entered the city by a ceremonial route, stopping along the way to pay their respects to the communal church of San Zeno. Perhaps most important to the culture-loving Veronesi was a remarkable system of public education at all levels and open to all classes.

In 1454 Venice signed a treaty with Milan that secured its newly won conquests in the Lombard plains and brought peace and a return of prosperity to the mainland. The first undefended country villas were built by the aristocracy. The wool industry revived, and mulberry trees were planted to meet a growing demand for Veronese silk. Contemporary descriptions are full of praise for the fruitfulness of the terrain: the famous vineyards, the infinite varieties of pears and apples, the forests of olive trees, medicinal herbs on the grassy slopes of Monte Baldo, wheat in the plains, flocks of sheep grazing in the meadows, the incomparable succulence of the river and lake fish. By 1500 the population of the city had grown to about 42 000, double its mid-century level.

The first century of Venetian control coincided with the rebirth of Italian interest in all things Roman. To have been a Roman city in the Renaissance carried immense prestige, and negotiations with Venice were coloured by a hidden agenda, about the cultural superiority of Verona. Venice called itself the New Rome. But it was not built on Roman foundations: it was built on mud, and it was a comparatively upstart, *nouveau-riche* and philistine society. Venice was only too willing to encourage Verona's intense but harmless pride in its ancient

In the 1460s the Torre dei Lamberti was raised from its Romanesque base and completed with a clock and Renaissance lantern.

Overleaf The Scala della Ragione (the Staircase of Reason) in the courtyard of the old communal palace was built in the late fifteenth century to give access to the law courts. It was, with the Loggia del Consiglio and the raising of the Torre dei Lamberti, one of the three major building projects initiated by the local government in the first century of Venetian rule.

lineage. Its rhetorical reply was that the ancient glory of Verona had been revived under the guidance and protection of the Most Serene Republic.

It was less easy to manipulate the real threat presented by the old German Imperial connection. By the end of the century the bourgeois and peasant classes had been converted to the Venetian system of government, which they recognized as the agent of their much enhanced well-being. The patricians, however, had not dissolved their long-standing ties with Germany. For them the Imperial Eagle emitted a glamour with which the enlightened and sensible Venetian polices could not compete.

In 1508 France, the Papacy and Habsburg Germany formed an alliance, the League of Cambrai, whose secret purpose was to dismantle the Venetian mainland empire. In the following May the League defeated Venice at the Battle of Agnadello. It was the first major reversal the Republic had suffered, and it was compounded when, before the month was up, Verona welcomed the occupying army of the German Emperor Maximilian I.

The City in the Early Renaissance

It is often claimed that the Scaliger centre was 'Venetianized' in the fifteenth century. And it is true that the Venetians, according to their usual practice, adapted existing buildings for their own use. The rectors took over Cangrande's palace and either added or enlarged its loggia; parts of the communal palace were given over to lawcourts and prisons; and, later in the century, the Venetian *capitano* moved into Cansignorio's fortress palace.

But the three major interventions that transformed the political centre were all initiated by the communal government and paid for by local taxes, raised with the permission of the *capitano*. These projects were realized only after years of careful consideration, prolonged debate, delays caused by financial set-backs and changes of plan. The result is one of the most successful, if peculiar, city centres in Italy. The retention of the fourteenth-century archways that link the buildings and give access to the Piazza dei Signori is a model of sensitive town planning. Structures of many different periods and types are united in a dignified harmony that is in satisfying contrast with the lively architectural farrago of the adjacent Piazza delle Erbe.

The Scala della Ragione, a handsome if bizarre throwback to a Venetian Gothic type of external staircase, was installed in the courtyard of the old communal palace after 1446. The Lamberti tower was raised from its striped Romanesque base to its present height of 83 metres — it is still the tallest in the city — and completed with its Renaissance belfry in 1463.

Finally, in the 1490s, the enlarged municipal council moved into new purpose-built offices opening on to the Piazza dei Signori through an open portico, the Loggia del Consiglio. This lovely, airy public loggia was a deliberately striking contrast to the fortified castles from which the last of the Scaligers had ruled. It signified the transference of power, under the benign supervision of Venice, from the tyrannous rule of the Scaligers to the people. Like Venice, where the Doges' Palace had been the earliest undefended government building in Italy, Verona was now thought to have a stable government that could afford to conduct its business in a headquarters that was freely accessible to its citizens.

The Loggia del Consiglio is the most beautiful quattrocento building in Verona, and the only one distinguished enough to be illustrated in most standard textbooks about early Renaissance architecture. Nevertheless, although it borrows some decorative features from the two Roman gates, it is by no means a perfect specimen of classical design. The axis of the arcade is punctuated in the centre by a pilaster, rather than broken by a wider interval that would have given it the symmetry on which classical purists of the period insisted. The arches are supported on full columns, a structural solecism according to followers of Alberti, who prescribed that columns should only be used to bear the load of entablature and wall.

But the Loggia is more then graceful enough to have prompted scholars over the last three centuries to search for the identity of its architect. None has ever been discovered. One of the councillors who served on one of the building committees that supervised its design and construction is named in a poem by his nephew as the architect. But the new government palace took more than forty years to build after it was first mooted in 1451; and the name most frequently invoked in the building records of successive committees as their master and guiding spirit is Vitruvius. His statue stands in the row of the other famous Romans who were thought to have been natives of Verona when they were placed on the roofline of the Loggia in 1492.

The exquisite Venetian Gothic Palazzo dei Merli at Pradelle di Gazzo Veronese was built in the early or mid-fifteenth century, probably for Zan Andrea Bennassuto Montanari, whose initials ZA MO are borne on the coat of arms over the door. The swallow-tail, or 'Ghibelline', battlements on the roofline served a genuine defensive purpose. It was not until Venice and Milan signed a peace treaty in 1454 that the Veronese aristocracy began to build undefended pleasure villas and to invest more extensively in farming. By the eighteenth century there were some 400 patrician villas in the territory. The Palazzo dei Merli is one of the few that are open to the public. Pradelle di Gazzo is about thirty-five kilometres south of Verona.

The Loggia del Consiglio was the most successful of the committee-designs raised in quattrocento Verona. Unlike Florence, Verona had no great banking families who were prepared to take adventurous artistic risks; there was no court, as at Urbino or Mantua, to which independent Renaissance princes could summon innovative architects whose style happened to appeal to them.

The committees who rebuilt Verona in the fifteenth century were drawn from a political and ecclesiastical establishment that was deeply imbued with humanist culture. But their architectural taste, like that of all committees, was conservative and eclectic. They continued to prefer Gothic shapes until after mid-century. And they never employed a professional architect who could translate their understanding of classical literature into the structural language of the new classical architecture. They relied instead on an abundant local supply of Lombard stone-carvers, who worked very much in the style of the Lombardi family then active in Venice, and on decorative painters who were good at illusionist architecture and scenes from Roman history and mythology.

Although the original frescoes of the façade of the Loggia del Consiglio have been lost, the building owes much of its charm to its richly and delicately carved marble facings. And the facings of the portals and windows of quattrocento churches and domestic houses are among the delights that await anyone who wanders through Verona's streets. By the end of the fifteenth century Verona was also the most painted city in Italy, and the epithet *marmorea* had been replaced by *urbs picta*, the painted city. The exterior frescoes have mostly faded beyond recognition or been repainted, although you can still see traces of fifteenth-century fresco under the eaves of some palaces. The clearest surviving example of fifteenth-century interior architectonic fresco is in the cathedral, where the elaborate and extensive painted frames of the nave chapels have recently been restored to something close to their pristine appearance.

The sixteenth-century art historian Giorgio Vasari describes a striking decorative scheme painted on three sides of a palace overlooking the Adige. It was 'executed partly in chiaroscuro and partly in colours. On the front, which looks towards the river, are combats of marine monsters; on another are battles of the Centaurs, with certain of the Italian rivers; and the third has two colourful

One of the side chapels incorporated into the walls of the Cathedral nave when it was re-built in the fifteenth century. The unusually elaborate architectonic frescos that frame the chapels are an interesting example of the Veronese love of decorative surfaces.

pictures, the subject of one, which is over the door, being a Feast of the Gods, and that of the other, the fable of a marriage between the Benacus (that is the Lago di Garda) and the Nymph of the Lake, Caris, from which marriage it is fabled was derived the birth of the river Mincio, which does in fact rise from the Lago di Garda . . .'

The taste for surface decoration was so strong in fifteenth-century Verona that it persisted for centuries. In the sixteenth century, Paolo Veronese, the most distinguished of the Veronesi 'decorators' who collaborated with Palladio, turned the tradition into high art.

Before 1450 there was more activity in church building than in civic and domestic building combined. This was partly because the bishops, who calculatedly happened to be Venetian throughout the century, were well placed to find money from Venice for improvements to religious structures. New churches were built, including the gaunt, routinely Gothic San Bernardino and Santi Nazaro e Celso. Earlier churches, whose fabric had been neglected since the last years of the Scaligers, were restored. The cathedral was thoroughly modernized, the walls of its nave being entirely rebuilt to incorporate rows of shallow absidal chapels. Sant'Anastasia, which had been left unfinished during the Scaliger rule, was completed in a faithful Gothic style according to the unrealized fourteenth-century plans. Its red-brick bell tower was raised in the 1460s, around the same time as the Lamberti tower, and still contributes the second tallest vertical accent to the skyline.

Many church interiors were transformed by a boom in the building of private chapels and altarpieces, which guaranteed wealthy families social prestige in this world as well as the next. Sant'Anastasia was the most fashionable address, but the character of the other great Gothic mendicant churches, San Fermo and Santa Eufemia, was also altered. Their perimeters bugled with new chapels, and the tall Gothic windows on their flanks that had previously flooded the interiors with light were blocked by altarpieces. Verona has the largest and most splendid Renaissance altarpieces in Italy — and the darkest church interiors.

Although no new church façades were built, existing ones were smartened up with new portals and windows. The mongrel additions to the façade of Santa Eufemia provide a striking example of the stylistic schizophrenia that persisted in Verona until late in the century. The portal makes a sycophantic curtsey to a Venetian Gothic shape that had gone out of fashion in Venice itself decades before it was applied

Frescoed house façades in Piazza delle Erbe. By the sixteenth century Verona had more painted façades than any other Italian city and was known as *urbs picta*, the painted city.

The church and bell tower of Santa Maria in Organo. The sixteenth-century stone façade is to a plan by Michele Sanmicheli but was never finished beyond its lower order. The bell tower was completed in 1535 to a design by Fra' Giovanni da Verona, who is better known as a master of intarsia work than as an architect.

here in 1486. The tall and very narrow flanking Gothic windows are topped by tiny architraves and pediments that make an attentive bow to Roman Verona, and particularly to the Porta dei Borsari.

Two portals erected in the first years of the sixteenth century demonstrate that serious structural classicism had by then arrived in the city and that a professional architect rather than a committee may have been involved in their design. The portal of Santa Maria della Scala is severely correct, and quite unlike anything previously seen in Verona. The portal of the Bishop's Palace was also, in its more graceful way, unusual in Verona at the time it was applied in 1502. It is flanked by paired columns on elegant high bases, and completed by an ample round-headed tympanum over a magnificent entablature. Some experts believe it might have been the work of Fra Giovanni da Verona, who was an architect as well as a master of perspective intarsia. His magnificent intarsia choir-stall backs in the church of Santa Maria in Organo include views of Verona as it looked shortly before the Imperial occupation. One of them shows the Renaissance bell tower he was designing for the same church. It was not actually raised, however, until after the Venetians returned to power in 1517.

1509–1630

As it is true that the city of Verona is very similar to that of Florence in position, manners, and other characteristics, so it is also true that in the one, as well as in the other, there have ever flourished men of the finest genius, and of the highest distinction in every vocation.

Girogio Vasari, *Lives of the Artists*, 1568

This most faire City . . . hath a pure aire, and is ennobled by the civility and auncient Nobility of the Citizens, who are imbued with chearefull countenance, magnificent mindes, and much inclined to all good literature.

Fynes Morison, who visited Verona in 1595

And happy was that foote that first could press
The flowry champain, bordering on Verona.

Ben Jonson, *The Case is Altered*, I. ii

Four of the intarsiaed choir stalls in the chancel
of Santa Maria in Organo. They were made by
Fra'Giovanni di Verona in 1491–9. The panel
second from the right portrays the bell tower
Fra'Giovanni designed for the church.

Niccolò Machiavelli, who was in Verona in December of 1509 observing the progress of the war between Venice and the League of Cambrai for the Florentine government, reported that although the aristocracy was wholehearted in its support for the League and the German occupation, the middle and lower classes were enthusiastically loyal to Venice. The war soon proved unpopular with all classes. War, as always, was bad for the agriculture, industry and trade on which the economy depended. The occupying armies, which were underpaid, robbed rich and poor alike. The Imperial bishop was oppressive and unpopular. There was a plague in 1511.

In August 1516 the Venetians, who were now allied with the French, began a siege of Verona, but the attack was interrupted in the autumn by a peace treaty with the League, whose members had fallen out among themselves. Verona was ceded to the French, from whom Venice had to buy the city for a high price. In the following January the Venetians were welcomed into the city by a procession of citizens crying 'Marco, Marco', and carrying lions of St Mark, the symbols of Venetian domination, that had been hacked down from public places and hidden during the occupation.

An Imperialist party continued to exist in Verona until the following century, and in 1525 there was a plot to overthrow the Venetian government. But Venice was by now on the alert for treason and had its instigator assassinated. Nor did Venice forget that its victory had been won on paper and was thanks to luck and diplomacy rather than military superiority. The refortification of Verona was given urgent priority. There was a plan to build a citadel against the citizens, who were tainted with collaboration despite the loyalty of the lower classes. But the native military architect Michele Sanmicheli, who was employed to supervise the fortification programme, argued successfully against an openly despotic measure that might have provoked rebellion.

The two branches of the Habsburgs now pressed on the very frontiers of the Venetian state: from Austria, just across the Alps, and from Milan, which was ruled by Habsburg Spain from the 1530s. The Venetian policy of maintaining peace through neutrality *vis-à-vis* the Habsbergs depended on the strength of its key cities, and particularly of Verona, which became the main army assembly base on the mainland. The return of prosperity, an inevitable consequence of peace for Verona, gradually reconciled the aristocracy to the heavy contribution

The church of Santa Eufemia is one of the three great Gothic mendicant churches – the others are Sant'Anastasia and San Fermo Maggiore – that were altered in the fifteenth century. The mongrel additions to the façade of Santa Eufemia are a striking example of the stylistic schizophrenia that persisted in Verona until late in the century. The portal, applied in 1486, is a Venetian type that had by then gone out of fashion in Venice itself. The flanking Gothic windows are topped by tiny pediments that were probably inspired by the Roman Porta Borsari.

the city and its territory were required to make towards the cost of refortification.

Towards the end of the century Italy began to drop out of European economic competition. Venetian trade in the Adriatic and Mediterranean became increasingly insecure as it was challenged by Dutch and English interlopers and threatened by privateering Turkish fleets. The economic base of the Republic switched from international commerce to domestic industries and farming. Verona was the major producer of silk and wool cloth; and its province was the largest supplier of agricultural produce in the Veneto, as it still is today. The population grew to 58 000 by the turn of the seventeenth century.

Although the Venetian Republic did not play a significant role in the Thirty Years War, it did support the northern Protestant Union, from which it had nothing to fear, against the Habsburg Empire. In the early summer of 1630 contingents of Venetian troops returning from a siege of Mantua were garrisoned at Verona. They carried with them a disease, the Great Plague of 1630, against which there was no defence and which determined the fate of the city more drastically than any war.

High Renaissance Architecture: Michele Sanmicheli

Three influential Renaissance architects were born in Verona in the fifteenth century: Fra Giocondo in 1433, Giovanni Maria Falconetto in 1468 and Michele Sanmicheli in 1484. Vasari wrote that the people of the Veneto were 'under an eternal obligation to these three most excellent architects', who were responsible for introducing it to what he considered to be the only proper way of building, that is according to the classical principles that had first been revived in his native Tuscany.

In their long and fruitless search for the architect of the Loggia del Consiglio some historians have settled on Falconetto, others on Fra Giocondo after whom the Loggia is still named in older guidebooks. The truth seems to be that neither they nor any other professional architect designed any building in fifteenth-century Verona. The young Falconetto did work in his native city as a painter; but he was exiled after the Venetians returned in 1517 because, according to Vasari, he had painted the Imperial coat of arms on all the public buildings.

Sanmicheli went as a young man to Rome where he studied and measured the antique monuments, admired the work of contemporary architects, particularly of Bramante, and was employed by Pope Clement VII, jointly with Antonio Sangallo, to inspect and construct fortifications throughout the Papal States. Vasari, who was his friend and whose long biography remains the main source of information about his life and work, said that he returned to the Veneto feeling homesick, and, out of professional curiosity, inspected the fortifications of Padua and Treviso with such close attention that the Venetians arrested him, interrogated him and were so impressed by his expertise that he was appointed to oversee the Republic's fortifications both on the mainland and overseas in Corfù, Crete and Cyprus. This makes him

The portal of the Bishop's Palace, applied in 1502, was one of the few confidently correct classical designs executed in Verona before the German occupation of the city in 1509. Its architect is unknown, but some experts have suggested that it may have been designed by Fra'Giovanni da Verona.

the only great Italian Renaissance architect who was exposed to ancient Greek buildings.

After his return from Rome in the 1520s and until his death in 1559 he designed for his native city some of the greatest masterpieces of the Italian High Renaissance. He was adept at all branches of architecture – military, civic and religious. The two great wings of his enceinte of walls determined the ultimate size and shape of the city. The city gates and the palaces that he built for the aristocracy resumed the tradition of showy, *avant-garde* building begun under the Scaligers. His forceful, masculine neo-Roman style cast the mould according to which Verona continued to be built throughout the next two centuries.

Sanmicheli's buildings are structured, as the architectural historian Howard Burns has put it, 'with a rigorous and clean-cut stoneyness like a dry-stone wall'. This high quality of articulation was made possible by the continuing presence in sixteenth-century Verona of very highly skilled Lombard stonemasons. Sanmicheli's father and uncle were both stonemasons from Lake Como; his father had worked on the Loggia del Consiglio.

His buildings are informed by many direct quotations from the local Roman monuments, which were of course much more complete at the time he was building than they are now, and were a source of great pride to his wealthy, cultivated, but politically impotent clients. But his sophisticated structural syntax is entirely that of his own time, and is in many ways the antithesis of pure classicism. One can only wonder how the loquacious Thomas Coryatt – who early in the seventeenth century described Sanmicheli's walls as 'the fayrest of all the Italian cities that I saw, and indeede fayrer than any I ever saw before in all my life' – managed to confuse his gates with the ancient Roman ones.

His enceinte of walls was up to date but not innovative. The bastions, which have been preserved, are modified versions of the pointed shape typical of the late fifteenth century, which he squattened to provide flanking fire along and adjacent curtain walls as well as top cannon firing across the surrounding countryside. But two of the gates, the Porta Nuova built in the 1530s and the Porta Palio of about twenty years later, are the most magnificent city gates built in Renaissance Italy. The bastions were never tested during the lifetime of the Republic, but the gates were a diplomatic as well as an aesthetic triumph: a reward from Venice to the citizens of Verona and its territory (who

Above The exterior façade of the Porta Nuova, one of the city gates built in the sixteenth century, after Venice regained control of Verona, by the great native architect and military engineer Michele Sanmicheli. The gate faced the plains to the south from which the city was most vulnerable to attack. (It is now opposite the main railway station.) Sanmicheli's gate consisted only of the central block. It was extended to either side in the nineteenth century by the Austrians, but the work was done so carefully that the differences between the sixteenth- and nineteenth-century sections are almost impossible to detect.

Below The exterior façade of Sanmicheli's Porta Palio, the gate from the south-west. Built in the 1550s, some thirty years later than the Porta Nuova, it is one of Sanmicheli's masterpieces and the most magnificent city gate built in sixteenth-century Italy.

were required to pay two-thirds of the cost of the fortification), they glorified the Imperial Roman lineage of Verona and emphasized the crucial role of the modern city in the defence of the most efficiently run empire since that of ancient Rome.

The Porta Nuova stands on the southern edge of the city, which was vulnerable to attack from the plain. Its vigorous rustication expresses its military role and its use as an emplacement for artillery. On the show side, facing the country, the rustication was originally confined to the central block, with its coupled Doric order framing an archway that echoes the arches of the Arena. The coupled Doric order is used to very different effect in the even nobler design of the Porta Palio, which was not intended as an emplacement for artillery. It articulation is subtler, its rustication flatter.

Of the private palaces Sanmicheli built for the Veronese aristocracy only one can be securely dated. This is the Palazzo Honorij, which was begun in 1555 for the family of that name, in Piazza Brà. The arches of its portico reflect those of the Arena, the monument around which the piazza revolves while their keystones are replicas of the head of Giovio Ammone (which is now preserved in the Maffei Museum across the square) and a bull's head from the Roman theatre.

The building records for Sanmicheli's other domestic palaces have been lost, and only two, the Palazzo Bevilacqua and Palazzo Lavezzola (now Pompei), are attributed to him on stylistic grounds by all experts. The Palazzo Bevilacqua has the most complex and elaborately decorated, as well as one of the most successful, palace façades of its period. The windows of the rusticated ground floor are framed by Tuscan pilasters; they rest on sphynx-shaped corbels and their keystones represent antique busts – a reference to the collection of real antiquities that was kept within the palace. The pinion of an eagle, the Bevilacqua emblem, is woven into the rich relief decoration of the main entablature. Although the *piano nobile* level takes its pediments and fluted Corinthian half columns from the Roman gates, the rhythmic organization of its windows, which are grouped into triumphal arches, is utterly unclassical and indeed unique for its time. The asymmetry of the façade, which has five bays to the right of the entrance and only one to the left, is almost certainly the result of its being unfinished.

The much quieter façade of the Palazzo Canossa, which stands across the street from the Bevilacqua, is traditionally attributed to Sanmicheli

The Villa Sarego at Santa Sofia di Pedemonte in the Valpolicella shows the influence Sanmicheli had on his contemporary Palladio. This was the only villa Palladio built for a Veronese patron and the only one he built in stone. It was begun around 1565, and remained uncompleted beyond one half of one courtyard.

on the grounds that Vasari mentions it among his works. The attribution has recently been questioned and there is a suggestion that its design may in fact be by Giulio Romano, whose Palazzo del Tè at Mantua has a similar three-bay centre.

The Palazzo Lavezzola, which is known to have been commissioned by that family in the 1540s (it is now occupied by the Natural Science Museum), has a fully rusticated ground floor and, on the *piano nobile*, fluted Doric half columns – like those of the Porta Palio but employed to more serene effect. It is a much more straightforward plan than that of the Bevilacqua, but whether this relative plainness is a consequence of more mature artistic economy or of the instructions of thrifty patrons is impossible to say. Vasari tells us that the Lavezzola was much commended in its day, and it remains Sanmicheli's most famous palace.

The round or octagonal shape of all Sanmicheli's churches and chapels, in Verona and elsewhere, recall buildings he had seen in Rome: the Pantheon and other ancient Roman mortuary buildings and Bramante's Tempietto. The Pellegrini Chapel, which is attached to the church of San Bernardino, may have been his first private commission after his return from Rome. It was ordered in the late 1520s by Margherita Pellegrini as a memorial to her son, Nicolò. Its architectural repertory is almost identical to the façade of the Bevilacqua, but to work the complex system of triumphal arches into a perfectly round space was an even more remarkable *tour de force*, 'a thing exceedingly difficult to do', as Vasari commented. The chapel was left unfinished, possibly because the client's money ran out. The drum and Pantheon dome, which were completed in the eighteenth century, explain the chapel's rather chilly neo-classical atmosphere.

Sanmicheli's last design was for the Madonna di Campagna, a pilgrimage church five kilometres south-east of Verona. Its tall, smooth cylindrical exterior is surrounded by a Tuscan colonnade and broken by a belt of Ionic pilasters framing the windows that light the drum of the dome, which has a spherical wooden outer shell. The octagonal interior has the architecural refinement one would expect from its architect, but the craftsmanship of the detailing is disappointingly crude. The foundation stone of the church was laid in 1559, the year of Sanmicheli's death. Its construction was supervised by Bernardino Brugnoli, a relative by marriage and one of several disciples who carried

The Palazzo Bevilacqua, on the south side of Corso Cavour, has one of the most complex and elaborately decorated façades of any sixteenth-century Italian palace. The fluted Corinthian half-columns and pediments of the *piano nobile* are quotations from the city's ancient Roman gates, but the organization of the windows, which are grouped into 'triumphal arches', successfully defies classical structural principles. Notice the high quality of carving: Sanmicheli's father was a stonemason who had worked on the Loggia del Consiglio, and skilled stonemasons were still plentiful in sixteenth-century Verona.

The sixteenth-century Palazzo Canossa, which stands on the north side of Corso Cavour (no. 44), has traditionally been attributed to Michele Sanmicheli, but some scholars now believe it may have been built to a design by Giulio Romano. The row of statues on the roofline are in a tradition that began in Verona with the Loggia del Consiglio.

Sanmicheli's Palazzo Lavezzola, or 'Pompei', on the eastern embankment of the Adige near the Ponte Navi, now houses the Science Museum. It was commissioned by the Lavezzola family in the 1540s and has always been one of Sanmicheli's most admired palaces. The design – a rusticated ground floor with fluted Doric half-columns on the *piano nobile* – is more straightforward than the earlier Palazzo Bevilacqua.

Overleaf The church of San Giorgio in Braida dominates the northern outer curve of the Adige. Its dome, bell tower and the gate in front of the church were built in the late sixteenth century to designs by Michele Sanmicheli. The church contains two masterpieces by native sixteenth-century painters: Paolo Veronese's *Martyrdom of St George* in the apse; and Girolamo dai Libri's *Virgin Enthroned with Saints* over the fourth altar on the left. The word *braida* is a corruption of the German *breit*, or large, and refers to the large open space in which the church was built. 'Brà', as in Piazza Brà, is a shortened form of the same word.

forward specific projects designed by Sanmicheli. The unfinished façade of Santa Maria in Organo, the dome and bell tower of San Giorgio in Braida and the bell tower of the cathedral were also built by other architects to the master's plan.

The most interesting and influential of Sanmicheli's immediate followers was his nephew Domenico Curtoni, who was born in 1556 and whose most prominent building is the Gran Guardia, on the southern perimeter of Piazza Brà, opposite the Palazzo Honorij, which influenced the design of its more grandiosely proportioned façade. It was commissioned by the Venetian *podestà* in 1609 for use as an arms drill centre and meeting place for the aristocratic military academy of cavalrymen, but work was suspended in 1614 and the building was not completed until the early nineteenth century.

An academy of music was also projected in the first years of the seventeenth century, and in 1604 Domenico Curtoni won a competition to build the headquarters of the Accademia Filarmonica just outside the southern entrance to Piazza Brà, a site for which Andrea Palladio had previously designed an enormous private palace that never got off the ground. Curtoni's severely majestic Palladian portico to the theatre closes the far end of the courtyard of the Maffei Museum.

Sanmicheli's immediate influence was not confined to his native city. The early palaces in Vicenza designed by his younger contemporary Andrea Palladio owe him an obvious debt. Palladio's brick-and-stucco villas for Vicentine and Venetian patrons are in a more personal vein. But for the Villa Sarego at Santa Sofia di Pedemonte in the Valpolicella, which was the only villa he built for a Veronese patron, he returned to Sanmicheli's example. It was begun around 1565, and only one half of one courtyard was completed. But its massive scale gives the impression that the Sarego, who had been ennobled by the Scaligers, were a race of giants. It is Palladio's only stone-built villa – the tufa was brought in ox-carts from quarries on the family estate – and its powerfully rusticated columns pay homage to the outer wall of the Arena as well as to Sanmicheli's Porta Palio.

Palladio (who refused to design fortifications on the high-minded excuse that cities should be defended by good government rather than by force) was a very different artistic personality from Sanmicheli; and their relationship was perhaps all the more mutually enriching for their differences. Sanmicheli's rigorous, allusive, finely crafted architecture has proved less adaptable than Palladio's more fluid – and less labour-intensive – style. There are 'Palladian' villas all over the western world, some of them masterpieces in their own context; and post-modern architects, whether or not they have ever visited the Veneto and seen the originals, feel free to play with 'Palladian' components. The 'Sanmichelian' style is arguably the more exciting of the two. To see what the adjective means, however, one must visit Sanmicheli's native Verona.

Above Palazzo Bentegodi Ongania in Via Leoncino. The monochrome frescoes on the façade were painted in 1560 by Battista del Moro. Via Leoncino was always one of Verona's wealthiest streets.

Below The Gran Guardia, on the southern perimeter of Piazza Brà, was designed by Domenico Curtoni, who was Sanmicheli's most talented and influential disciple. It was commissioned by the Venetian *podestà* in 1609 for use as an arms drill centre and meeting place for the aristocratic military academy of cavalrymen; but work was suspended in 1614 and the building was not completed until the early nineteenth century.

4   Modern Verona

We think, and rightly, of Verona as a city of romance, a place inviolate in our dreams, consecrated for ever by the greatest of poets, the home of two people who possibly never existed, but who are much more real to us than most of those who cumber the world . . . Such is Verona as she appears to us in our day-dreams; but what is the real Verona?

Edward Hutton, *Venice and Venetia*, 1911

The gateway to the enclosure around the church of Santi Nazaro e Celso is known as the portal 'of the sheets' and is a rare example in Verona of the rococo style. The otherwise sober and correct Doric architecture is gracefully mocked by elegantly draped stone cloths tied around the shafts of its columns. It was made by an otherwise obscure stonemason in 1688.

In the spring of 1630 north Italy was visited by the most calamitous of the plagues it had suffered over the centuries. In Verona, where the first case was recognized in late May, the infection was intensified by troop movements. By the end of June two to four hundred people were dying there each day. When the disease finally subsided in October 1631 some thirty thousand citizens, more than half the population, were dead, and the proportion of dead to living was even higher in the countryside.

The survivors, looking back on the false sense of security that they had enjoyed less than two years previously, were struck with the guilty conviction that their city had been visited by divine retribution. Agriculture, industry and commerce were at a standstill. The recession persisted into the next century. Economic recovery was delayed by a fall in the price of grain and by competition from the more efficient open markets of northern Europe. The panic-response was to charge excessive duties on goods entering the city, which only made the situation worse. Many merchants, who had been able to count on 20 per cent profits before 1630, were bankrupted.

In the early eighteenth century the territory between the Adige and Mincio rivers was a theatre of the wars of Spanish and Polish succession. The Venetian lion snarled and rattled its sabres: troops were recalled from the overseas empire and stationed in Verona. But although the Republic did, for the time being, succeed in retaining its key mainland cities, the venerable stance of peace earned through neutrality was beginning to look more like a policy of peace at almost any price. It was also evident to politically aware observers throughout

Europe that the famous Venetian constitution which had served the Republic for nearly a thousand years was in need of a thorough overhaul.

One proposal for constitutional change was penned from Verona. Its author was the remarkable scholar, archaeologist and man of letters, Francesco Scipione, Marquis of Maffei, who was born in Verona in 1675 and became one of the most energetic exponents of the ideals of the European Enlightenment. The complete edition of his published writings runs to twenty-eight volumes. In the 1730s he travelled in northern Europe where he was impressed by the parliamentary democracies of Holland and England, and returned to Italy hoping to stir up the apathetic Venetian regime with an argument for greater decentralization of power. He suggested that the Venetian Senate, which was closed to all but Venetian aristocrats ennobled before the fourteenth century, should be opened to representatives from the subject cities.

Maffei's proposals were ignored in Venice. (They were not published until 1797, which was, ironically, the year when the Republican government that had failed to take his advice finally collapsed.) But his rational, utilitarian reformist theories had a profound effect on his native Verona, which, under his leadership, became the *avant-garde* centre of reformist Enlightenment ideas in the Veneto.

When Maffei died in 1755 the recession had lifted. Land reclamation and improved methods of agriculture made farming a more profitable activity than ever. The aristocracy, which owned nearly 50 per cent of the land, were once again prosperous. The scientific emphasis of Maffei's theories was carried forward by a college of civic and military engineering founded by Venice in the Castelvecchio and by an agricultural academy – both open only to the sons of patricians and high government officials. Verona was content. The egalitarian ideals of the French Revolution made less of an impact in Verona than in other north Italian cities.

In the spring of 1796 French troops led by Napoleon Bonaparte swept into north Italy striking at the Austrians, who were the chief opponents of the French revolutionary goals. Bonaparte stood for municipal autonomy and an end to foreign rule; and he received not inconsiderable support from many Italians, especially in the Austrian-dominated Lombard cities. Verona was less receptive, and even the few

Bernardo Bellotto (1721–80) painted seven views of Verona. This detail from the one now in Powis Castle, Wales, shows the hill of San Pietro as it was in the late 1740s when Bellotto was living in Verona. The castle on the hill was built by the Visconti in the late fourteenth century. It was demolished by the French in the early nineteenth century and replaced in the 1860s by the Austrian barracks that completes the view today. Photograph: The National Trust Photographic Library.

local French partisans were soon alienated by the barbaric behaviour of the young, untrained, trigger-happy French troops who occupied their city in June.

Resentment mounted until the following Easter when it exploded without warning into a miniature revolution. It was sparked by the old rallying cry, 'Viva San Marco!' Groups of citizens banded together and fought so furiously that the French troops were driven from the city centre for three days. The Pasque Veronese, as the Easter uprising was immediately dubbed by the European press, was an almost identical replay of the end of the Imperial occupation three centuries previously – except that this time Venice was far too confused and lethargic to do more than chide its loyal subject for wasting blood and compromising the policy of perfect peace.

Fifteen thousand French soldiers surrounded the rebellious city. The instigators of the Easter uprising were rounded up, sentenced at mock trials and shot. Less than a month after French-style municipal government had been forced on Verona at bayonette-point, Bonaparte fulfilled his famous promise: 'I will be an Attila to the state of Venice'. The Most Serene Republic surrendered to Attila with barely a shot fired in anger.

In the next years Verona passed back and forth between French and Austrian control. In 1801, after the peace of Lunéville, the city was split between the Austrians, who took over the left bank of the Adige, and the French, who held the right bank. In 1805 Verona was absorbed into Napoleon's Kingdom of Italy. In 1814 after Napoleon's retreat from Moscow and his convulsive defeat at the 'Battle of the Nations' near Leipzig, the victorious allies, Russia, Prussia and Austria, restored the Austrian presence in northern Italy.

The Napoleonic period had not been without benefits for Verona as for the rest of the Italian Kingdom. The price of agricultural produce continued to rise while the sale of ecclesiastic and state property enabled a new bourgeois class to invest in cultivated land. Nevertheless, the Austrians were welcomed in Verona as liberators. The French atrocities during the Pasque Veronese had not been forgotten. The Habsburgs, although foreigners, were foreigners with whom Verona had long, close historic ties and whose representatives were temperamentally more in tune with Verona's conservative military and mercantile establishment.

The Ponte delle Navi as painted by Bellotto in the mid-eighteenth century and as it is today. The Gothic bridge shown in the Bellotto was demolished in the late nineteenth century when the embankments were strengthened after a flood and an arm of the Adige that had formed an island in the river was filled in. Photograph (*above*): The Bridgeman Art Library.

Verona was made the command base of the Austrian armed forces in Italy, and a show-case for the efficiency of administrative and legal procedures which the Habsburgs believed would at last bring order to the unruly Italian peninsula. In the winter of 1822 Verona was chosen as the site of one of the periodic summit conferences that were intended to preserve peace and the balance of power in post-Napoleonic Europe. The Congress of Verona was the glittering event of the diplomatic and social calendar, attended by the crowned heads and greatest statesmen of eleven nations (the most popular with the crowds were the Emperor Alexander of Russia and the Duke of Wellington).

The Congress lined the pockets of many aristocrats who let their palaces at vast rents to visiting dignitaries. But it exhausted the municipal coffers and left the city with a sense of post-party depression. It also outraged those foreign liberals who supported the nascent underground movements for a free and unified Italy. Byron, a vociferous supporter of Italian independence, reacted with bitter sarcasm:

> Thrice blest Verona! since the holy three
> With their imperial presence shine on thee!
> Honour'd by them, thy treacherous site forgets
> The vaunted tomb of 'all the Capulets;'
> Thy Scaligers – for what was 'Dog the Great,'
> 'Can Grande,' (which I venture to translate,)
> To these sublimer pugs?

Byron spent his happiest hours during the Congress talking with his friend John Cam Hobhouse about Catullus, Dante and Shakespeare; they carried off a chip of red marble from Juliet's tomb as a souvenir. For Byron, as for many politically engaged foreign liberals of his generation, Italy's humiliating subjection to a foreign monarchy gave extra spice to the contemplation of the country's more glorious historical and literary associations.

In Verona, the pervasive military presence and the compliant municipal government made that contrast all the more poignant. It was one of the few Austrian-run Italian cities where the neo-Guelf movements for independence barely stirred, and where the tricolour was never raised during the insurrections against Austria of 1820 and 1831. Even the revolution of March 1848 – when Venice briefly

Right One of the water entrances to the late-eighteenth-century customs house on the Adige near San Fermo. The customs house was the last public building project initiated before the collapse of the Venetian regime in 1786.

Far right The portal of Palazzo Serego-Aligheri, designed by the neo-classical architect Luigi Trezza, was applied to the earlier palace in 1782. The rusticated Ionic columns are a late-eighteenth-century translation of the massive columns Palladio had designed for the same family at the Villa Serego.

re-established itself as an independent Republic – never got out of hand in Verona. Indeed it was from the garrisons of Verona that that revolution was finally crushed.

As the Austrian grip on Italy tightened, Verona was transformed into an immense military camp and supply centre. By the late 1830s, 10 000 citizens, one-fifth of the total population, were employed in the construction of fortresses and other military buildings. The wool and silk industries died out for lack of manpower. Troops stationed in the city often outnumbered the resident population. Even the 'sacred shrine' of Romeo and Juliet was used as a conscription centre.

Nineteenth-century Verona had a double identity. The real Verona was one of the most heavily fortified cities in Europe. But there was also the Verona that epitomized the northern European Romantic ideal of Italy. For many visitors from across the Alps Verona was not merely the threshold of Italy: it was Italy's heart and soul, a sleeping beauty which could be awakened by the kiss of cultivated understanding and imagination.

And for none more than John Ruskin, who loved Verona longer and more passionately than any other foreigner and whose feelings for it conditioned the taste of subsequent generations of visitors. It is largely due to Ruskin's preference for the Gothic that cultivated British tourists, until quite recently, ignored Renaissance and post-Renaissance Verona. Ruskin made some twelve visits to Verona, the first in 1835 when he was 16, the last in 1888, twelve years before his death, Although he sympathized with the aims of the Risorgimento, he was obsessed with the monuments of the Ghibelline city. While his wife Effie flirted with Austrian officers, he sketched the Scaliger Verona with an almost voyeuristic attention, sometimes as though its remains were half alive.

After the 1848 revolution, Verona became the civic capital of Habsburg Italy, its main communications centre, and the bulwark of the 'quadrilateral' of Italian cities – the others were Mantua, Peschiera and Legnago – which Austria fortified in order to defend its dominion over an increasingly restive peninsula. The investment in the quadrilateral drove the Habsburg treasury into debt, and all for a war that it was doomed to lose, and whose decisive battle was not even fought on Italian soil.

In 1866 an Italian army, with the blessing of Italy's ally, Prussia, advanced on the quadrilateral. It was checked at Custoza. But before the Austrians could follow up this victory they were diverted by Prussia's own northern drive against them through Bohemia. It was the Austrians' defeat at Sadowa that forced them finally to vacate the quadrilateral and yield the Veneto to united Italy. After Verona was annexed to Italy in October 1866 the Italian state maintained Verona as a garrison against Austria, which retained the Trentino, until the end of the First World War.

In the last years of the Second World War Verona was made the capital of the German puppet Republic of Salò and was the scene of

Right Pen-and-ink drawings of six villas in Verona by Scipione Maffei, from *Verona Illustrata*, published in 1734. The drawings demonstrate both the changes and continuities in the style of palace façades from the sixteenth-century designs of Michele Sanmicheli through to those of the eighteenth century.

Far right Sanmicheli's Porta Nuova drawn in 1839 by D. Macatta before the outer façade of the gate was extended by the Austrians. Photographs: The British Architectural Library, RIBA, London.

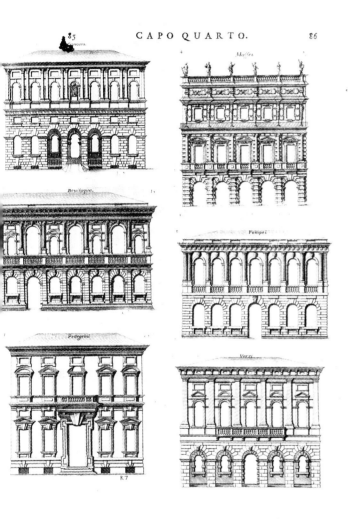

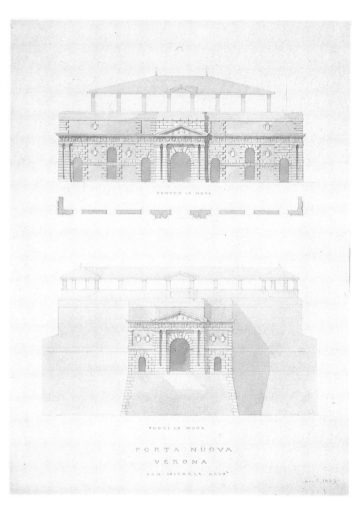

Mussolini's hysterical executions of his former fascist supporters. The economy and morale of the city picked up rapidly after the war. And Verona is today, once again, north Italy's major supplier of agricultural produce and one of the wealthiest mercantile centres in Europe. Unfortunately, however, the crossroads location and old entrepreneurial spirit have attracted a flourishing drugs trade, a problem which the municipal government, a socialist-Christian democrat coalition, has been slow to tackle, merely shifting the pushers from Piazza delle Erbe to the inner suburbs.

Verona is one of the seven provincial capitals of the Veneto, of which Venice is the regional capital. But Verona has retained a sense of assured autonomous identity that Venice, through the decline of its resident population and its reliance on tourism, has lost. The Veronesi are more likely to define their collective civic personality by contrasting it with that of Padua. Padua, as they say, was Pompey's city, Verona was Caesar's; Padua was Guelf, Verona Ghibelline; Padua was a city of bankers, Verona of merchants and soldiers. Go-ahead Padua, the university city, has always been eagerly receptive to new ideas. Conservative Verona, where there are more good antiquarian book-shops than in most cities twice its size, has found nourishment in historic continuity.

The Modern Cityscape

A map of Verona is open, the small strange city;
With its river running round and through, it is river-embraced,
And over this city for a whole long winter season,
Through streets on a map, my thoughts have hovered and paced.

Henry Reed, 'A Map of Verona', 1946

Sanmicheli was to Verona what Palladio was to Vicenza. His style was so richly suggestive and so suitable to the spirit of the place that it remained the cardinal reference point for successive generations of architects in his native city. Some emphasized his classicism, others his mannerism. But in the seventeenth century the fashion for baroque architecture was checked as much by his example, and by that of his follower Domenico Curtoni, who died in 1627, as by the after-effects of the plague.

No professional architect worked in the city for a century after the plague. As in the fifteenth century, patrons who wished to build in the modern style relied on talented local craftsmen. Their experiments with the baroque and rococo are interesting as isolated examples, but they made no significant impact on the character of Verona. The busiest of the stonemason/builders were the members of the Miglioranzi family, who kept their workshop in the Arena. Bernardino Miglioranzi was responsible for the most inspired and bizarre baroque work of art in Verona: the extraordinary Porta dei Bombadieri in the Tribunal

Ruskin's preference for Verona's Gothic monuments conditioned the taste of cultivated British tourists until quite recently. His watercolour sketch of the Cansignorio mausoleum in the Arche Scaligeri is dated 1851–2. Photograph: The British Architectural Library, RIBA, London.

courtyard. Commissioned in 1689 by the civic volunteer gunnery company, its heavily loaded military imagery is based directly on illustrated title-pages of contemporary treatises on artillery.

The earliest of the baroque private palaces, and by far the oddest, is the eccentric Palazzo Turchi on a corner of Via San Cosimo. It was begun in 1571, the year in which Venice claimed a victory over the Turks at the Battle of Lepanto. The busts of Turkish captives which terminate the herms flanking the portal are references to the Turchi family's role in congratulating the Doge on his visit to Verona in that year. They are trophies of war and emblems of tamed barbarianism, as well as puns on the family name. The palace aroused the anger of a gang of citizens who carried off some of the statues and subjected them to a ritual 'execution'. Nothing remotely like this palace was ever again seen in Verona.

The most conspicuous and distinguished of the seventeenth-century private palaces is Palazzo Maffei, which stands at the north-west head of Piazza delle Erbe. According to Scipione Maffei, who came from a collateral branch of the family for whom it was built, the palace was designed in Rome, and it certainly conforms more closely to contemporary Roman places than to those built in the Veneto. It was first projected in 1626, but construction was delayed by the plague and not completed until the 1660s.

Its ground-floor arcades, which were reserved for shops in the original plan, were occupied after 1691 by a consortium of shopkeepers that modelled itself on the union previously established on the Rialto bridge in Venice. The six statues on the balustrade represent the gods and goddesses of Mount Olympus. The beautiful interior stone

staircase, which winds in an airy, uninterrupted spiral from the shop level to the top storey, is one of the most exciting things in Verona.

Some of the religious orders were enriched by public and private donations made during and after the plague, and many old churches were updated with unsuitably elaborate new altarpieces that conformed to the dramatically explicit style prescribed by the Counter-Reformation. The two important new churches were the Jesuit San Sebastiano and the Theatine San Niccolò. San Niccolò, as it stands today, is in fact a combination of both these church buildings. Its imposing Sanmichelian façade belonged originally to San Sebastiano, the rest of which was demolished during the Second World War. Its classically proportioned but sumptuously decorated interior – the high altar was designed by the great Theatine architect and philosopher Guarino Guarini – is the most architecturally serious baroque church interior in the city.

The portal of the enclosure around the church of San Nazaro e Celso is, by contrast, a pleasingly frivolous architectural joke. The otherwise entirely sober and correct classical arrangement is mocked by lengths of stone cloth elegantly tied around the shaft of each of its paired Doric columns. The portal 'of the sheets', as it is commonly called, is the masterpiece of the otherwise obscure stonemason Antonio Saletti, who made it in 1688. His delicately carved 'sheets' look like a flirtation with the rococo style.

That, however, was a tendency that was soon stamped out in his native city by Scipione Maffei, who likened baroque and rococo exuberance to the frills and furbelows worn by ridiculous fops. Maffei intended to make Verona an exemplary ideal city of the future, a Utopia of the Enlightenment, where the educated élite would make themselves responsible for cultivating the minds of the untutored proletariat. He was an ardent supporter of the dramatic arts, public education and commercial independence, as well as being a playwright himself; and he believed that these essential urban activities should be given prominent and equal architectural status.

The enfeebled condition of the Venetian central government made self-definition imperative: Verona was a mercantile/aristocratic society with vigorous Roman roots; its new architecture should express that autonomous identity. Classicism, for Maffei, meant a return to first principles. Republican Rome was the source and symbol of the reason and order that were the only bases for healthy civilization. His *Verona*

The tomb of Gugliemo da Castelbarco above the cemetery gate of Sant'Anastasia. Ruskin called it 'the most perfect Gothic sepulchral monument in the world'. The black-and-white photograph by a member of Moritz Lotze's studio shows the tomb from inside the cemetery as Ruskin knew it and before it was subjected to a crude restoration in the late nineteenth century. The restorers replaced the original canopy with the weather-proof one seen in the modern photograph, which is taken from outside the cemetery. Photograph (*far left*) © Umberto Tomba.

illustrata, published in 1732, is partly an exhaustive archaeological survey of Roman Verona, partly a polemical plea for a return to the values of Republican Rome. The alien poetic depravities of the baroque, as realized in Verona by 'idiot bricklayers', were corrupting and incomprehensible to the ordinary man in the street. Even Sanmicheli was condemned for his free departures from the strictest possible interpretation of Vitruvian principles; and Maffei used his considerable local influence to exclude any architect who did not share his rigorously dogmatic urban ideology.

He persuaded his fellow dilettante-aristocrat, Count Alessandro Pompei (1702–72), to turn from portrait painting to the study of architecture. Pompei schooled his eye by making analytical drawings of Sanmicheli's buildings, and became the chief architect of Maffei's programme of urban renewal. Their museum, completed in 1745, was one of the first purpose-built public museums in Europe. It deliberately turned the tradition of the aristocratic gallery of antiquities inside out by displaying its collection of classical sculpture in the open air, sheltered by a peristyle built out from the façade of the Philharmonic theatre. A collection of inscriptions, which was meant eventually to comprise a 'stone library' of samples of all known languages, was also displayed.

The complex was subsequently so frequently and insensitively re-managed that its architectural merits are now impossible to judge. The architecture was in any case intended to be subservient to the objects on display. Goethe commented unfavourably on the dissonance between Pompei's low, functional Ionic peristyle and the giant columns of Curtoni's Palladian façade. But the clash was certainly less strident when the courtyard was visible from the street and Piazza Brà.

The most impressive expression of the Maffei/Pompei ideology, the Customs House which they built in the old gardens of the church of San Fermo, is probably the most interesting, and certainly the most unusual, complex of eighteenth-century buildings in the Veneto. Fortunately, it is also much better preserved than the Maffei museum. It went up in the space of only one year, 1745–6, and without the permission of the aggrieved Venetian authorities, who pointed out that its peremptory architecture seemed unnecessarily handsome given its stated purpose, which was merely to receive goods entering the city by river and road from Bolzano.

Above Moritz Lotze's photograph of the Austrian army bakery at Santa Marta, which was built in 1865. It was the last, and the most architecturally interesting, of the military buildings with which the Austrians surrounded Verona during their occupation.

Below The Arena photographed by Moritz Lotze in the late 1850s. The ground-floor arcades had been used as shops and workshops for many centuries. Photographs © Umberto Tomba.

The church of Santa Maria in Organo was originally approached by a bridge from an island formed by a branch of the Adige. This photograph, one of a series of Verona during and after the Austrian occupation by the brilliant Prussian photographer Moritz Lotze, was taken before the natural arm of the river was filled in in 1882. Photograph © Umberto Tomba.

It was, of course, precisely intended as an emblematic challenge to Venetian interference with Verona's commercial independence. The spacious rectangular courtyard, which was meant to be one of the main venues where merchants could meet informally, was modelled on the Roman Forum as described by Vitruvius. The Tuscan order of the double-loggiaed peristyle, as quoted from the Arena and Roman theatre, was an emphatic re-affirmation that these buildings belonged in Verona and nowhere else.

Maffei's Utopian experiment died with him in mid-century, after which the aristocracy concentrated more on building or enlarging their private palaces and villas than on supporting public works. You can see good late eighteenth-century patrician palaces in Via Leoncino (which had always been the richest street), Corso Porta Borsari, Piazza Brà and Via Emilei/Via Forti. Palazzo Emilei, which houses a gallery of modern art, stands on the site of Ezzelino da Romano's tower house. The present neo-classical palace was designed in 1780 by Ignazio Pellegrini for Count Pietro Emilio Emilei. Bonaparte took it as his residence during the Italian campaigns of 1796–7.

The two most prominent architects active in the late eighteenth century were Adriano Cristofali (1718–88) and Luigi Trezza (1752–1823). Cristofali was a disciple of Pompei and went to Rome under his guidance. But he abandoned his mentor's fastidious purism and reverted more openly to the example of Sanmicheli. He exercised a strong influence on the next generation and particularly on Trezza, who also visited Rome, where he met Canova and other pioneering exponents of international neo-classicism. He made drawings of Sanmicheli's buildings, which provide reliable records of those which have subsequently been altered. The palaces he built or adapted in Verona are Palazzo Orti-Manara in Corso Porta Palio (1784), Casa Faccioli in Piazza Brà (1790) and Palazzo Serego-Alighieri in Via Leoncino.

The rusticated Ionic columns of the portal of Palazzo Serego-Alighieri are a late-eighteenth-century translation of the massive columns Palladio had designed for the same family at the Villa Serego. Palladio's columns, as we have seen, were themselves references to the Arena and to Sanmicheli's interpretations of the Arena. Trezza's portal was applied to the Serego palace in 1782. In the same year the riverside section of the Customs House was completed. The rusticated columns of its four gates frame arches whose keying reflects that of the windows of Sanmicheli's Palazzo Lavezzola-Pompei on the opposite bank of the Adige. Four years later, when the French occupied the city, the architectural dialogue about Verona's identity and its relationship to its Roman and Renaissance ancestry came to an abrupt halt.

The French initiated a programme of road widening, of which the most lamented victim was the Arco dei Gavi, dismantled in 1805 along with a section of the Castelvecchio clock tower to which it had been attached. The castle ditch was also narrowed by five metres where it ran parallel with the road. A bump on the surface of Corso Cavour indicates the original position of the Arco. Napoleon's excuse for its removal was that it impeded his troop movements, but the people of Verona took it as an act of revenge for their sullen attitude to the French regime. Napoleon also stole from the Maffei Museum some of its prize antiquities, which are still in the Louvre.

Under the French and Austrians Trezza drew up grand, visionary and unrealized projects for organized public spaces, including a plan to make Piazza Brà the 'Napoleonic forum'. But the French post-Revolutionary vogue for imposing order on cities never made much impact on Verona, except in Piazza Brà which, in the early nineteenth century, assumed its definitive appearance and became the hub of the modern city. In 1812 the southern section of the piazza was cleared with the demolition, regretted by nobody, of a late-eighteenth-century hospital. Curtoni's Gran Guardia was completed in 1821, in time for the Congress of Verona.

Finally, in 1840, the neo-classical municipal palace (as it now is) filled the south-east section of the piazza. This uninspired monster is chiefly interesting for its size, which rivals that of the Arena, and as a demonstration of how completely divorced Verona had become from its native classical tradition. Its routine international neo-classicism is as dead and out of keeping with its context as the parliament building of a banana republic. And yet the intentions of its architect, Giuseppe Barbieri, who drew up the proposal in 1819, were eminently sensible. The palace was supposed to serve as a grain market, annual trade fair, military training centre, as well as housing restaurants, a theatre and other public spaces – all activities that had traditionally taken place in the piazza. The deep, intrusive curve of its rear end respectfully echoes the curve of the Arena. Which just goes to show that sensible and rational planning does not always produce the most pleasing results.

The most important buildings of nineteenth-century Verona were erected outside the city by the Austrians after their refortification programme began in earnest in the 1830s. The Austrians strengthened Sanmicheli's walls and the existing city gates, and surrounded Verona with a far-flung double ring of fortifications. They built some three dozen military buildings, including twenty-seven barracks – that is nearly as many as there were churches in the historic centre – with an emergency capacity of about 25 000 men and 5000 horses. The infantry barracks on the hill of San Pietro, which had previously been occupied by a Visconti castle demolished by Bonaparte, is only the most visible from the city centre. It was erected in 1856 to house 463 men.

The neo-medieval Franz Josef I Arsenal at Campagnola (1854–61) was modelled on the Arsenal at Vienna, but today looks more like a gloomy spa hotel. It is much less interesting than the army bakery of Santa Marta (1865). This was the last of the Austrian military buildings, and, although its neo-medieval architecture refers to a Germanic rather than local tradition, it is also the most architecturally refined. The rhythmic arrangement of its pitched and stepped rooflines, grouped round-headed windows, and the vertical thrust of buttresses break up the masses of the façades and give the exterior elevations an energetic and stylish individuality.

The historic centre – as one can see from Ruskin's drawings, and from the brilliant and moving photographs taken by the Prussian photographer Moritz Lotze who worked in Verona on and off between 1854 and 1866 – was scarcely touched under the Austrians. The enormous cost of the fortification programme, which involved, as well as bricks and labour, paying heavy compensations for compulsory land purchase, left nothing over for urban improvement. Neglect is often a positive force for preservation. But to be fair to the Austrians it should be said that preservation orders blocked many potentially ruinous modernizations. And when the Austrians did adapt an historic monument, as they did Sanmicheli's Porta Nuova, it was done with such skill and sensitivity as to be barely detectable to anyone who has not compared its present appearance with Trezza's drawings of the original.

The decaying condition of the inner city was, for Ruskin at least, part of its charm. He drew a branch of wild fig sprouting from the façade of Sant'Anastasia, and made a study of the grasses and moss growing

between the stones of the Ponte Pietra. When he returned to Verona three years after its annexation to the united Italy he found a statue of Dante, one of the symbolic heroes of the Risorgimento, standing in Piazza Signori, which had been officially renamed Piazza Dante. He was just in time to make drawings of his favourite monuments before they were enthusiastically restored by a well-meaning municipal government that had ceased to understand them. Ruskin foresaw, accurately, that the new bourgeois urban values would inflict more damage than the Austrians. All the most important buildings – including the Loggia del Consiglio, which was stripped of the last fragments of its original frescoes, and the Arche Scaligeri – were subjected to radical restorations.

In September 1882 the Adige overflowed its banks, as it often had over the centuries. It was an unusually severe flood; but the remedy, which totally altered Verona's relationship to its river, was far more drastic than the natural disaster. The Acqua Morte, an arm of the Adige which had looped away from the left bank embracing an island in mid-river, was filled in. Its course is traced by the street known as the Interrato dell'Acqua Morte. On the right bank old palaces which had risen directly out of the water, as in Venice, were torn down to make way for river walkways, for which the example of Paris had set a fashion in late-nineteenth-century cities. The only positive outcome of these interventions was the unearthing of a large number of Roman statues and inscriptions.

In the early years of this century the municipal government became increasingly conscious of a duty to preserve and display to the public – which included the growing numbers of tourists that began to flock to Italy – its city's rich material heritage. The Roman theatre, which had been privately owned since 1833, was purchased by the city in 1904, its remains were rearranged to make them more comprehensible, and in 1923 the Archaeological Museum installed in an old convent above. The annual summer opera season in the Arena opened in 1913 with a production of *Aida*.

After the First World War, when Verona ceased to be an important garrison city, the Castelvecchio, released for the first time in its history from its military function, was restored and opened in 1926 as a museum. The *reggia* was accurately returned to its original aspect as a signorial residence. Two façades of the courtyard of the barracks side were rebuilt incorporating elements of palaces demolished during the post-flood reconstruction of the embankments. In 1932 the Arco dei Gavi was resurrected on its present site overlooking the Adige next to the Castelvecchio.

The motives for restructuring the Maffei Museum were less public-spirited, and the results far less successful. In 1927 the Philharmonic Society hired the architect Ettore Fagiuoli to 'adapt' the complex in order to release part of the site for resale. Pompei's peristyle was dismantled and the columns and trabeation reused to build a courtyard eleven metres shorter and twelve metres narrower than the original dimensions. The corners of the east end were rounded to form a bayed shape which was meant to soften the effect, but which of course merely made the clash between the peristyle and atrium of the theatre all the more strident. Fagiuoli extended the design of Cristofali's portico of the theatre, which had been left unfinished in the late eighteenth century, along Via Roma. Fagiuoli was also, incidentally, the architect of the post office building in Piazza Indipendenza.

In the last years of the Second World War Verona suffered some thirty major bombardments. All the bridges were mined or bombed. The city was rebuilt after the war with considered care and accuracy by an enlightened administration, which also had good connections in Rome. Some bomb damage was, inevitably, exploited by property speculators, but this was far less of a problem in Verona that in, for example, Padua, which, like London, has been more disfigured by post-war speculative development than by the war itself. In Verona most new building has been relegated to the suburbs – the Borghi – immediately outside the old city walls. One of the few modern buildings in the historic centre is, ironically, the Hotel Due Torri, put up in 1958 in Piazza Sant'Anastasia on the site of the Gothic palace where Ruskin always stayed.

Perhaps the single most exciting architectural achievement of the post-war years was the exemplary restructuring of the Castelvecchio Museum by the great Venetian architect Carlo Scarpa (1906–78). It was carried out in the late fifties and early sixties when the high standard of craftsmanship that was one of Scarpa's trademarks was still readily available. In every respect, from its detailing to its lucid and beautiful organization of the exhibition spaces, it remains one of the most successful and influential conversions of its kind in Italy. Scarpa's

Banca Popolare di Verona in Piazza Nogara was his last building and one of his least remarkable. It was finished after his death by other hands and at a time when the tradition of fine craftsmanship was beginning to die out, even in Verona.

Verona is by no means immune from the conflicts of interest that make sensible town planning difficult in so many prosperous north Italian cities, particularly those of socialist-Christian democrat government. Traffic management is chaotic. A section of the historic centre is closed to traffic for part of each day, but elsewhere cars clog the narrow streets and endanger the foundations of old buildings. The permanent collections of museums, which are amongst the most distinguished in Italy, are neglected in favour of irrelevant 'popular' exhibitions.

Nevertheless, restoration continues to be carried out to a high standard. A list of scholarly investigations and restorations under way or completed in the last decades of the twentieth century would include, as well as excavations of the Roman city and parts of the medieval city, restorations of the fourteenth-century Arche Scaligeri, the fifteenth-century Loggia del Consiglio, the sixteenth-century Porta Nuova and Palazzo Canossa, the seventeenth-century Palazzo Maffei and portico of the enclosure of San Nazaro e Celso, the eighteenth-century Customs House at San Fermo and the Maffei Museum. When in the course of restoration or routine repairs some fragment from the past is uncovered, every effort is made to preserve at least a section of it.

The aim, in other words, is unbiased respect for each of the successive layers and different architectural scripts of one of the most densely crowded urban palimpsests in Europe. It is a challenge that requires fine judgements backed by expertise, scholarship and of course money. Verona is further blessed with a healthy temperamental mix of Germanic efficiency and Italian flair. Its refusal to give in to the cynical neglect and the greedy development that disfigures so many other great cities in the name of progress is a demonstration that enlightened preservation, far from dooming a modern city to the ranks of the dead, for-tourists-only museums, can be a source of vitality and renewal.

View over the roofs of Verona,
taken from the Lamberti tower.

Travellers' Information

Transport

Verona is easily accessible from all directions by motorways, good secondary roads, railway and air. The airport Valerio Catullo at Caselle di Sommacampagna (tel: 513039) takes scheduled flights from Rome and Munich and some charters from London. The main railway station Porta Nuova (tel: 590688) is 1 km south of Piazza Brà. The city centre is closed to inessential private traffic but is small enough to be explored on foot. Taxis are readily available but expensive. City buses are efficient and inexpensive. Bicycles can be rented from the Noleggio Biciclette in Piazza Brà at Interrato Torre Pentagona 13 (tel: 596852).

Tourist information and sightseeing

Tourist information offices are at Piazza Erbe 42 (tel: 30086) and Via Dietro Anfiteatro 6/b (tel: 592828). The opening hours of museums and monuments are generous by Italian standards, usually from 8 am to 6.45 pm. Churches, as usual in Italy, close for a long mid-day break, from noon until 4 or 5 pm. Verona's churches are very dark. Bring a supply of 200 lira coins to operate the lights that illuminate the major works of art.

Events

Operas are performed in the Arena from late June to September. For information or tickets, contact the Ente Lirico, Arena di Verona, Piazza Brà 28, 37100 Verona (tel: (045) 8003204). There is also a summer festival of plays, mainly by Shakespeare, performed in the Roman theatre. Agricultural and livestock fairs are held frequently throughout the year.

Hotels

Verona is well supplied with hotels in all price categories. Most are clean, efficient and friendly. The following are all in the historic centre.

The best and most expensive hotel in Verona is the modern Due Torri, Piazza Sant'Anastasia 4 (tel: 595044; fax: 8004130; telex: 48054).

Well-managed, comfortable hotels in the upper-middle price range include: Accademia, Via Scala 12 (tel: 596222; telex: 480874); and Colomba d'Oro, Via C. Cattaneo 10 (tel: 595300; fax: 594974: telex 480872). Two sensible and moderately priced commercial hotels are: Bologna, Piazzetta Scalette Rubiani 3 (tel: 8006830; fax: 8010602; telex: 480838); and Giuletta e Romeo, Vicolo Tre Marchetti 3 (tel: 8003554).

Aurora, Via Pellicciai 2 (tel: 59471) is an inexpensive small hotel with views over Piazza delle Erbe.

Restaurants

Verona is the food and wine capital of the Veneto, and the best of the restaurants generally maintain a standard that justifies their very high prices. The traditional specialities – such as potato gnocchi and *peara*, a sauce made with marrow bone – that once sustained the poor are difficult to find in which is now one of Europe's richest cities; but the local produce – fresh lake and river fish, and seasonal vegetables and fruit – remain outstanding.

There is a row of useful bars, pizzerias and restaurants along the Liston in Piazza Brà. All put tables outside in fine weather. Olivo (Piazzo Brà 18, tel: 30598) also has a large, bright interior room where excellent snacks, pizzas and full meals are efficiently served.

The following are the most gastronomically ambitious and expensive of the city's restaurants. It's a good idea to book in advance for all of them, particularly during the summer and trade fairs.

Arche, Via Arche Scaligere 6 (tel: 8007415), closed all Sunday and Monday lunch, is the best of the fish-only restaurants.

Il Desco, Via Dietro San Sebastiano 7 (tel: 595358), closed Sunday, does unusual pasta dishes and stays open after the opera.

Dodici Apostoli, Corticella San Marco 3 (tel: 596999), closed Sunday dinner and all Monday, has a charming frescoed interior.

Nuovo Marconi, Via Fogge 4 (tel: 595295), closed Sunday, is an intimate and unpretentious restaurant that serves fastidiously prepared dishes based on seasonal local ingredients.

Sympathetic but less expensive restaurants include: Rubiani, Piazzetta Scaletta Rubiani 3 (tel: 8006990), closed Friday. Re Teodorico, Piazzale Castel San Pietro (tel: 49990), has a terrace from which you can enjoy a spectacular view over the city.

VeronAntica, Via Sottoriva 10/a (tel: 80014124), closed all Sunday and Monday lunch.

Further Reading

The following are the printed sources on which I have drawn most heavily.

Albertini, Bianca; Bagnoli, Sandro, *Scarpa: l'architettura nel dettaglio* (Milan, 1988)

Barker, Nicholas (ed.), *In fair Verona: English travellers in Italy* (Cambridge, 1972)

Brugnoli, Pierpaolo; Sandrini, Arturo (eds.), *L'architettura a Verona nell'età della Serenissima*, 2 vols. (Verona, 1988)

Brugnoli, Pierpaolo; Marinelli, Sergio; Prandi, Alberto (eds.), *Lotze: lo studio fotografico 1852–1909*, cat. Museo di Castelvecchio (Verona, 1984)

Cipolla, Carlo, *La Storia Politica di Verona* (Verona, 1954)

Lorenzoni, Giovanni, 'Problemi di storia urbanistica altomedievale: l'esempio di Verona', *Arte Documento*, no. 2, 42–5 (Venice)

Magagnato, Liscio, *Arte e civiltà del medioevo Veronese* (Turin, 1962)

Manasse, Giuliana Cavalieri (ed.), *Il Veneto nell'età romana*, vol. II. esp. Manasse, G. C., 'Verona' (Verona, 1987)

Marinelli, Sergio; Mazzariol, Giuseppe; Mazzocca, Fernando (eds.), *Il Veneto e l'Austria: vita e cultura artistica nelle città venete 1814–1866*, cat. Palazzo della Gran Guardia, Verona (Milan, 1989)

Marini, Paola (ed.), *Il Museo Maffeiana riaperto al pubblico* (Verona, 1982)

Marini, Paola (ed.), *Palladio e Verona*, cat. Palazzo della Gran Guardia, Verona (Venice, 1980)

Mullaly, Terence (ed.), *Ruskin a Verona*, cat. Museo di Castelvecchio, Verona (Verona, 1966)

Norwich, John Julius, *A History of Venice* (London, 1983)

Simeoni, Luigi, *Verona: guida storico-artistica della città e provincia* (Verona, 1909)

Vasari, Giorgio, *Lives of the Artists*, various editions (1568)

Index